George Henry Needler

Richard Coeur de Lion in Literature

George Henry Needler

Richard Coeur de Lion in Literature

ISBN/EAN: 9783337205089

Printed in Europe, USA, Canada, Australia, Japan

Cover: Foto ©Thomas Meinert / pixelio.de

More available books at **www.hansebooks.com**

RICHARD COEUR DE LION

IN LITERATURE.

VON

DR. GEORGE HENRY NEEDLER.

LEIPZIG
GUSTAV FOCK
1890.

I.
Introduction.

The life of Richard Coeur de Lion fell in the midst of a period in which, more than in any other in the history of Western Europe, men gave themselves up to the delights of adventure and the sturdy joys of living; when, more than at any other time, life was made a romance. It was not a time, indeed, of such unclouded sunshine as we might be led to suppose from the poetry of the Troubadours alone, which was then at its zenith, but the spontaneous freshness of this poetry, pre-eminently lyric as it was, shows us at every step that the poetic and the prosaic, the romantic and the every-day, aspects of life were more nearly one than they ever were before or have been since. And Richard Coeur de Lion was at once one of the most important figures in the political world of that time, and one of the time's most typical representatives.

Though king of England from 1189 to 1199 Richard spent scarcely six months of his reign on the island, a fact, however, which must not mislead us to believe that his sympathies were entirely estranged from this the principal part of his kingdom. England was then, as far as the court and the upper classes were concerned, as thoroughly French as France itself. From the year 1066, when William duke of Normandy defeated Harold the last of the Saxon kings at Hastings and made himself king of England, French influence had ruled supreme. And Richard Coeur de Lion was even less English than his predecessors since the conquest, spent less of his time on the island, and bestowed less care on its government. But this was chiefly owing to the fact that the exigencies of the time called him elsewhere, and forced him to devote nearly all his energies to maintaining his possessions in France intact. England in the meantime, safe from the attacks of his enemies, and with its peaceful population already at work laying the foundations of future mercantile prosperity, was principally useful to Richard in furnishing him with the means of carrying on his expensive wars and exploits in France and in countries farther away. In spite, however, of his seeming neglect of this portion fo his subjects, he was held by them in the very highest esteem, and it was they who longest perpetuated his valorous deeds in their poetry. In as short a period as about a century after his death Richard Coeur de Lion had become almost as much a mythical personage in epic poetry as Roland and Charlemagne. This quick process of heroification, if one may use the word, was begun by Norman-French romancers and, probably about the beginning of the fourteenth century, taken up by versifiers in the English language; the course of political events at that time favored the process, and with the rapid fusion of the numerically small, but politically great, element of Norman-French conquerors with the main body of the English people, Richard became transformed by the singers into a national English hero, whose chief glory was his life-long antagonism to the French. The fact that he was French himself and had only been the rival and enemy of another king in France, had in the course of a hundred years faded away to a dim tradition, and Richard in the heroic poetry of the fourteenth century was only the brilliant counterpart of the Edward of the then national struggles with a later French rival. But in the meantime the political relations of France and England had very greatly altered, and „France" had come to denote an altogether different tract upon the map of Europe. Here it is not necessary to follow the course of these political changes, but some account of Richard Coeur de Lion's life and sphere of action will form the most fitting standpoint from which to view the tortuous path he wandered, or rather has been made to wander, in the world of literature, where his figure has been constantly re-appearing, from the time of his contemporaries amongst the Troubadours almost down to the present day.

In 1168, when only 12 years old, Richard was made by his father Henry II. of England duke of Aquitaine. Right at the beginning of his activity as a ruler, he gave evidence of that severity in his nature which often amounted to cruelty, and his vassals were continually rising in rebellion against him. Almost the whole western half of the France of the present day formed then a part of the dominions of the kings of England, whose reigns were one long series of wars with the kings of France their neighbors and rivals to the east. The family of Henry II., too, was often disturbed by domestic broils, and in the campaigns of this king against Philip August of France the sons of Henry, with Richard at their head, often went so far as to range themselves on the side of their father's enemy. From his early years Richard distinguished himself before all others by his bravery and daring, and when in 1189 he succeeded his father upon the throne of England, he set to work to secure his possessions in France from the attacks of Philip. On August 13th of this year he went to England and had himself crowned there, but returned on December 12th to France. He soon made peace with his rival Philip, and in the following year the two kings joined in a common crusade to the Holy Land. After many adventures in Sicily and Cyprus Richard landed in June 1191 before Acres, where Philip had arrived a couple of months before. The old feud between the two leaders soon broke out again, and after a stay of only four months in Palestine Philip sailed for home on a plea of ill health. Richard carried on the war against the Saracens until the end of the following year, winning a wide-spread glory by his feats of arms, and before leaving Palestine concluded a three years' peace with the sultan, the heroic Saladin. On the journey homeward, being wrecked on the northern shore of the Adriatic, he endeavored to pass through Central Europe in the guise of a palmer, but fell into the hands of Leopold duke of Austria upon whom he had once vented his wrath in Palestine, and was by him given over to the emperor Henry VI. who kept him prisoner from December 1192 till February 1194. The required ransom of 100,000 marks was raised — almost entirely in England — and after regaining his freedom, Richard proceeded on his way to his island kingdom. There he remained barely two months, and crossed over to Normandy. England he never saw again. The last five years of his life were principally taken up by renewed wars with Philip, until in 1199, while engaged in the siege of the castle of Chaluz, which belonged to one of his rebellious vassals, he met his death by an arrow from the walls.

The most characteristic feature of Richard's character was his dauntless bravery, and in the numerous wars which, as we see, took up the greater part of his time, he found ample opportunities for brilliant exploits. But it was not in achievements on the battle-field alone that he was the first knight of his day. There was a milder side to his nature, namely, the virtue of splendid generosity, which showed itself especially in assistance to the singers whom he attracted to his court, and in whose art he took more than a passive interest. For Richard Coeur de Lion himself holds a place, if only a very modest one, amongst the poets of his day; and ranks amongst the most meritorious of the princely patrons of poetry in that period, on account of the active assistance and favor he extended to so many of the foremost poets of the Provence.

II.
Richard and Contemporary Troubadour Poetry.

The closing years of the twelfth century saw the highest development of lyric poetry in the Provence, and contemporary with Richard Coeur de Lion flourished the greatest of the Troubadours. Marcabrun 1140—1185, Bernart of Ventadour (about) 1148—1195, Peire Vidal 1175—(about)1215, Bertran of Born 1180—1195 (time of greatest activtiy), Guiraut of Borneil 1175—(about)1220, Rambaut of Vaqueiras 1180—1207, Gaucelm Faidit 1190—1240, all flourished during his life-time, and, as will be seen, several of these and others of only less distinction were more or less intimately connected with Richard and his court, whether as political enemies or as partakers of his bounty.

Richard doubtless inherited his love for poetry and the talents which enabled him to be not only a lover of it, but an active practiser of the art, as was the case with so many of the princes and nobles of that day. His mother was the celebrated Eleanor of Aquitaine, herself a grand-daughter of one of the first Troubadours, William IX. earl of Poitiers. She was a constant friend of the poets, and Bernart of Ventadour, who visited her court while her husband, afterwards Henry II. of England, was yet only duke of Normandy, honored her in his verses. We can with certainty suppose that this was only one example out of many, and that during Richard's early years the poets were always welcome guests at his father's court, and by none seen more gladly than by the young prince. We are told by Richard's biographer, Roger of Hoveden, that, when made by his father duke of Aquitaine, he caused verses to be written in his honor — Roger even calls them „begged-for poems", emendicata carmina — and attracted French singers and gleemen by gifts to his court, in order that they might proclaim his praises in public places. It would seem that he attained his object in this rather peculiar way, for „it was soon said everywhere" — so continues the biographer — „that there was none such as he in the world". By another historian, Richard, a Canon in London[1]), in his Itinerarium Ricardi, an account of Richard's deeds in Palestine, we are told that the king was there attacked by duke Henry of Burgundy in indecent songs, and that he replied in songs of a similar sort. The anecdote, too, concerning the discovery of Richard's place of imprisonment by the French minstrel Blondel, though lacking an actual basis in history[2]), nevertheless points to what was probably a well-known fact, that Richard had at least made some practical efforts in poetry. And of this we have surer evidence in the manuscripts which have preserved the poetry of the Troubadours, for here we find two poems ascribed to Richard I. of England.

The first of these is a complaint in prison, which is preserved only partially in the Provençal text, but perfectly in the French, a proof that it was originally written in the latter language.[3]) — When imprisoned in Germany Richard was wont to pass the time in performing feats of strength for the guards and such other recreations of that kind as were allowed him. Besides this he found a consolation in composing verses and singing. But in spite of the joviality of his character we can easily imagine him becoming impatient under the confinement and breaking out into such

---

1) And not Geoffroi de Vinisauf. See Stubbs' introduction to his edition of the Itinerarium in „Chronicles and Memorials of Gt. Britain and Ireland".

2) See Raumer, Geschichte der Hohenstaufen III, 33.

3) Mahn, Werke der Troubadours I, 129. The Old French text is printed by Leroux de Lincy, Recueil de chants historiques français I, 56.

complaints as are contained in the following verses, which date from the winter of 1193—94, shortly before his release, and of which I will give a metrical translation.

A prisoner boots it naught to tell his wrong,
As mute endurance doth to grief belong,
Yet may a man for comfort make a song:
Poor are their gifts, tho' rich my friends and strong,
Shame be to them that I two winters long
   For ransom lie in bonds.

Now well must all my knights and barons know
In Gascony, England, Normandy, Poitou,
That I count not the poorest serf so low
To leave him ransomless imprisoned so;
This say I not contempt on them to throw,
   But still I lie in bonds.

This truth doth now itself to me commend:
A prisoner, like a dead man, hath no friend.
If they their gold and silver will not spend,
Hard fate for me; yet will a worse attend
Themselves in the reproach after my end,
   They left me thus in bonds.

No wonder is it that my heart is sore:
My lord[4]) to turmoil now my land gives o'er,
And thinks upon the solomn oath no more
That we together to th' Almighty swore;
Yet know I well 'twill not be long before
   I shall be freed from bonds.

Companions whom I loved, and cherish still,
Of Cahors and of Perche, I live until
'Tis sung that they no longer oaths fulfil,
Tho' knew they ne'er in me a recreant will.
The deed of caitiffs, should they treat me ill
   While I remain in bonds!

---

4) The king of France.

Well, too, know they of Anjou and Touraine,
Those mighty knights to whom I call in vain,
That hostile hands their lord far off detain.
Aid me they might, — but that they count no gain;
They're men renowned in arms, yet feel no pain
    That I am still in bonds.

O Countess, sister[5]), for thy weal doth pray
Thy captive king; may guard thee God alway
    For whom I am in bonds.
Let Lewis' mother still at Chartres stay,
    — For her no prayer resounds.

The second poem by Richard is a sirventes addressed by him to the Dauphin of Auvergne and Gui of Auvergne, and has reference to a quarrel which arose between them and Richard in 1196 after the latter's return to his French possessions. By the treaty of Louviers Auvergne had been handed over to Philip in exchange for another province. With this change of masters the counts of Auvergne were not at all satisfied, and with right, for their new lord bought a castle in Auvergne and deprived the Dauphin of the town of Issoire. Richard promised assistance to the brothers in their opposition to Philip, but seems to have in reality left them sadly in the lurch, so that nothing remained for them to do but make peace with Philip as best they could. When after a time the French king made an attack on some of Richard's possessions, the latter had even the audacity to call upon the Dauphin of Auvergne and his brother to support him, which they naturally refused to do. At this juncture Richard composed, in French, the following sirventes[6]), of which I also give here a metrical translation.

---

    5) Richard's sister Johanna, first married to William II. of Sicily, and afterwards to Raymond, Count of Toulouse. Hence called Countess.
    6) Mahn, Werke der Troubadours I, 129.

Dauphin, I will you arraign,
You, and with you too Count Guy,
For in the years till now gone by
Doughty warriors were ye twain,
Kept your oath of loyalty,
And were as faithful unto me
As once the Wolf unto the Fox,
— Your likeness in the fallow locks.

Your aid from me ye both withold
Lest the guerdon be too low,
Since at Chinon now, as ye know,
Lies no silver and no gold;
A king that's rich is now preferred,
High in arms, that keeps his word:
And I'm a coward, niggardly,
So that ye look no more to me.

Once more of you I would inquire:
Issoire, if good of it ye hear?
Will ye still go to chase the deer,
And there your soldiers still to hire?
But one thing shall ye constant know, —
Tho' ye thus do break your vow,
A warrior of undaunted mind
In king Richard shall ye find.

I saw at first your liberal ways,
Largesses in full abound;
But occasion soon ye found
Such mighty castle towers to raise
That now no gifts, no wealth is spent
In festive court or tournament:
But this trouble may ye spare,
For Langobards[7]) the Frenchmen are.

---

7) The Lombard merchants were notorious for their dishonesty and treachery.

Go, sirventes, send I thee
Unto Auvergne; say thou from me
To both the Counts, that should they e'er
Seek peace, may God o'er them have care.

A faithless henchman, what if he
Lacks the sense of loyalty?
Henceforth let him but beware
Lest harsher fate he have to bear.

The Dauphin, who also has his place among the poets of that time, answered king Richard in a similar sirventes[8], in the course of which he speaks of the latter as one „whom the villanous Turks feared more than a lion".

Though from these two poems of king Richard that have been preserved we are not justified in ascribing any high degree of poetic talent to the author, yet even these are sufficient proof that he was by no means a stranger to the flourishing art; and they make it easy for us to realize the joy he found in the productions of the poets, and the liberality with which he befriended so many of them and attached them to himself. Indeed, the personality of Richard Coeur de Lion is closely bound up with the contemporary Troubadour poetry in its highest representatives.

Peire Vidal, that peculiar combination in one person of the court jester and the court poet, was for a time personally connected with Richard, and in all probability accompanied the latter as far as Cyprus on the way to Palestine. In the poetry of this Troubadour Richard is mentioned occasionally, but only in passing; and from one of his later poems[9] we may infer that the earlier friendship between king and poet had come to an end, for here the poet expresses his opinion that, if the emperor were to set Richard free, now that he has him in prison, the English would only ridicule him for doing so.

---

[8] Mahn, Werke der Troubadours I, 131.
[9] Mahn, Wke. d. Troub. I, 227.

Folquet of Marseilles also enjoyed the favor of Richard, and in several of his songs gives expression to his gratitude and esteem. Two years before Richard really entered upon the crusade, he was accused from some quarter of unwillingness to take part in the rescue of the Holy Sepulchre, and Folquet of Marseilles took up his defence, as we see from the following words from one of his poems[10]): „But he who blamed the good king Richard, of whom I sing, for not having departed then, defends him now, for one sees that he held back in order to better go forward . . . . . It is clear from his taking the cross that I say the truth, and now it is seen that I did not then speak falsely." At the close of a second poem[11]) Folquet expresses a wish that Limousin (a portion of Richard's dominions as duke of Aquitaine) were nearer his home, „in order that I might oftener see my liberal and powerful lord."

Of still greater interest is Richard's relation to one of the greatest of all Troubadours, to Bertran of Born, whose poetic activity reached its climax in the years 1180—1195. Bertran stood on very intimate terms with the family of Henry II. of England, and had for each member of it a nickname. Richard, in whose nature there were so many contradicting characteristics, and who could in few respects be with certainty reckoned upon, appears in the poems of this Troubadour as Oc e No, Yes and No. In the neverending quarrels between Richard and his brothers Bertran would, according to the circumstances, take part first with one and then with the other, or even caused additional troubles by stirring up the sons against their father — a crime for which Dante thought fit to place him in one of the lowest circles of hell.[12]) While Richard ruled as duke of Aquitaine in his earlier years, Bertran more than once experienced the severity of his sway; but the poet, who was

---

10) Mahn, Wke. d. Troub. I, 322.
11) Mahn, Wke. d. Troubad. I, 323.
12) Divina Commedia, Hell 28.

noble knight as well, was himself no submissive spirit, and bravely opposed his domineering feudal lord by word and sword. In one of his sirventes[13]) of this period he bestows upon Richard the far from flattering appellative „Poitevin glutton", and at other times many similar ones. Later on the poet became reconciled with the prince, and visited his father's court in Normandy in 1183. From this time forward he appears as a true adherent, but is nevertheless not always content with his feudal lord. „Never", he says[14]), referring to Richard, „will a court be perfect where there is no jesting and laughing; a court without gifts is nothing but a park of barons." In another place, however, he speaks in quite a different tone of Richard's liberality, and compares him in this respect with the niggardly Philip of France, a comparison which was made by many of their contemporaries. The following from a sirventes[15]) by Bertran is very characteristic: „King Philip loves peace more than the good man of Carentrais, while my Yes and No (Richard) wishes war more than does one of the Algais (well-known robbers)." And again[16]): „Richard catches hares and lions, and turns not aside for plain or wood; he binds them two and two by his strength so that none dare move; and from now on he thinks to catch the mighty eagles with merlins, and with buzzards to put the hawks to shame.

„King Philip hunts with falcons his sparrows and little birds, and his men dare not tell him the truth, for he is little by little letting himself be despoiled by Richard &c."

At no time was Bertran of Born a servile flatterer, and however much he sings Richard's bravery and noble qualities, he „presents him", as he says, „with many a cutting word."

---

13) Mahn, Wke. d. Troub. I, 278.
14) Mahn, Wke. d. Troub. I, 291.
15) Mahn, Wke. d. Troub. I, 298.
16) Mahn, Wke. d. Troub. I, 299.
17) Mahn, Wke. d. Troub. I, 275.

In the years 1180—1200 flourished the Troubadour known by the name of the Monk of Montaudon. This peculiarly favored individual tells us how that, Enoch-like, he frequently visited Paradise during his life-time, and in his poems he gives accounts of the conversations that he there held with the Almighty. From the following words, taken from one of his poems, we can see that the good Monk, like so many of his brothers in the poetic art, had received favor and gifts from Richard. The Lord speaks to him[18]: — „Monk, thou hast done ill, that thou didst not at once go willingly to the king to whom Salaros (unknown reference) belongs, who was so much thy friend; that he may ever be gracious unto thee. Ha! how many good marks sterling he has lost in gifts to thee, for he raised thee from the dust."

Of Arnaut Daniel, held by Dante and Petrarch for the greatest of the Troubadours, and who was celebrated for his difficult rhymes, a story is told, according to which he had a contest with a minstrel at Richard's court, upon which occasion the king played the part of judge. In his later years Arnaut Daniel found himself in needy circumstances, and Richard was one of the princes who responded to his plea for support.

Guiraut of Borneil speaks of king Richard shortly after the latter's death in the following words:[19] — „I believe not that since the time of Charlemagne was there born a king celebrated and extolled for so many glorious deeds." And the poet then goes on to lament that the names of such great men should so soon be forgotten.

But none of his contemporaries has paid Richard such a noble tribute as Gaucelm Faidit in his well known elegy[20] upon the king's death. As this poem forms such a fitting close to the references to Richard in Troubadour poetry, I will give it in full in translation.

---

18) Mahn, Wke. d. Troub. II, 64.
19) Mahn, Wke. d. Troub. I, 201.
20) Mahn, Wke. d. Troub. II, 92.

Sad lot it is, that of the blow most sore,
The greatest grief, alas! e'er fate did bring,
O'er which henceforth my plaint must ever pour,
I now am doomed to sing anew the story;
For he who was of heroes chief in glory,
The mighty Richard, England's valiant king,
Is dead! O Heaven, what source of sorrowing!
What awful word! What horror death to dare!
His heart is hard this grief unmoved can bear.

Dead is the king! In many a hundred year
Such mighty man was not; no, ne'er was seen,
Ne'er lived a man the world might call his peer,
So generous, brave, of such a matchless name;
Tho' Alexander Persia's king o'ercame,
Such gifts he spent not, nor such meed, I ween.
Not Charles was his compeer, nor Arthur e'en:
He all the world compelled — let truth be said —
One half to honor him, the other dread.

Strange is it that in this false age 'tis thought
A wise man should to noble deeds go forth,
Since upright deed or word availeth nought.
Who then would strive to live one noble hour?
And death has shown us now how great its power,
Has robbed in this one blow the best from earth,
All honor, what ennobles, what hath worth.
And since we see for nought 'twill turn aside,
We, too, should less in fear the end abide.

How, valorous Prince, alas! shall live again
The joy in sword and lance and kinghtly state,
What castle halls resound to festive strain,
Since thon, the bloom of kinghthood, absent art?
For what shall now the desolate have heart
Who served thee faithful at thy board but late,
And now in vain upon thy bounty wait?
What shall they do, who owe to thee alone
Their all, but wish their days like thine were done?

A life of shame that's worse than death is then
Of those thou leav'st behind the hapless lot;
Whilst Heathen, Turk and Persian, Saracen,
Who trembled at thy name of mortals most,
Will go their way, and from th' inflated host
The Sepulchre will be more dearly bought;
God wills it thus, for if his will 'twere not,
And thou, O Sire, hadst thou but life again,
In Syria would they longer not remain.

Small hope I have the holy grave to see
By king or prince from hand of heathen wrung;
Yet ought they all that follow after thee
And fill thy place, thy noble spirit know;
How, too, thy valorous brothers twain lived so, —
Count Geoffrey and the royal ruler young;
Who now will take his place you three among,
In truth a heart must have unerring bent
On noble deeds, and all on good intent.

O heavenly Father who dost mercy show,
Who art true God and man, true life, I pray
Forgive him, for he oft forsook thy way;
Look not, O Lord, upon his deeds of shame,
Remember only how he served thy name.

    With Gancelm Faidit ends the list of the more important Provençal poets amongst Richard's contemporaries, who were more or less closely connected with him, and in the life-time of Gaucelm Faidit, in fact, began the decline of Troubadour poetry in general. In the poems of the Troubadours who flourished after Richard's death we find references to him from time to time, but nothing that is not in keeping with the picture drawn by his contemporaries. The younger Bertran of Born, a son of the famous poet already mentioned, says in a sirventes[21]) which he addresses to John, Richard's brother and successor upon the throne of

---

21) Diez, Leben u. Werke d. Troub., 426.

England: — „Would he but remember his predecessors, well might he hang his head in shame for giving over Poitiers and Tours to Philip without a struggle. All Guienne mourns for king Richard, who devoted so much gold and silver to their defense; but our present lord (John) seems not to give them a thought." The poetry of the Troubadours was devoted almost exclusively to persons and events of the present, and with the death of a prince, a knight or a fair lady poems ceased to be written in their honor, and their names sunk into oblivion after the succeeding generation. As far as the poetry of the Provence is concerned, such was the case with Richard. During the years from 1169, in which he entered upon his active career as duke of Aquitaine, until his death in 1199 as king of England, lived and flourished the greatest poets in the annals of the Provence, and few princes of that period were so often the subject of their verses as Richard. He was the ideal knight, and in his person were united, to a high degree, the weaknesses as well as the virtues likely to draw the poets to him, and arouse enthusiasm in them. In the political world he was an important figure, and we have seen that he also, on account of his intimate personal relations with many of the poets themselves, played a considerable part in the history of the poetry of that period.

From the many adventures of Richard's life, and his exploits on the field of battle and elsewhere, marvellous enough in themselves, arose in course of time stories much more marvellous still, in which fact had lost itself in fiction. From the realm of actual history, by a gradual transition through chronicles partaking of the nature of both extremes, we pass now to the realm of the completely legendary.

III.
Metrical Chronicles and Metrical Romances.

1. Ambrosius' Histoire de la guerre sainte.[22])

Already during his life-time Richard appears in a poem of quite a different kind. A certain Ambrosius, concerning whom little is known, wrote — probably in the year 1196 — an account of the third crusade in rhyming couplets of 8 syllables. The poem, which consists of some 12000 lines, possesses next to no poetic worth, but is highly valuable from a historical point of view, as, with the exception of a few Anglo-Norman works, it is the earliest French account of contemporary events extant. The author professes to have witnessed the meeting of Philip and Richard in Normandy, the crowning of Richard in London, the march of the crusaders from Vezelay to Lyons, and their sojourn in Messina. As a faithful adherent of Richard, Ambroise always places his master in the most favorable light. „The earl of Poitiers, the valiant Richard, would not be wanting in God's need and call for help; he took the cross out of love for him. He was the foremost of all the noble men of the lands we yet know." The poem is a very matter-of-fact account of historical events. In Messina, says Ambroise[23]), began the jealous hatred of Richard on the part of Philip, „which lasted all his life. There originated the war that laid Normandy waste." The close of the poem contains a short reference to the war of retaliation undertaken by Richard against king Philip after his return to France in

---

22) Printed in part in Monumenta Germaniae historica XXVII, 532 ff.

23) ll. 825 ff.

1194. The homeward journey and Richard's detention in Germany are only mentioned in passing. This work of Ambrosius was soon after its completion translated into Latin by Richard, a prior of Holy Trinity at London.

2. Konrad of Würzburg's Turnei von Nantheiz.

Next in order of time comes a work by an important German poet of the 13th century, the Turnei von Nantheiz of Konrad of Würzburg, by which we see that Richard was by no means to disappear from the world of poetry with the decline of the Troubadours. This Tournament of Nantes is the first example of the class of heraldic poems, and is also written in 8-syllabled couplets. It is a pure fiction of the poet, and has no historical event for its basis. In a great tournament which is supposed to have been held at Nantes, Richard king of England appears as the hero of the day who outshines all competitors by the brilliance of his feats in the lists. „He was true and steadfast, powerful, noble and mighty; there lived not his equal within the circle of many lands." Many celebrated kings and princes come to the tournament, but Richard surpasses them all in strength and skill. When he entered the ranks of the combatants „he clove the throng, just as a keel cuts through the sea-foam". In the closing verses the poet does not forget to tell us that Richard, among his many virtues, had also that of liberality to the „travelling folk", the minstrels. By far the greater portion of the whole poem is taken up in descriptions of the magnificent attires of the various participators in the tournament.

This poem, which dates from about the middle of the 13th century, that is, only 50 to 60 years after Richard's death, is evidence that he was known beyond the confines of his own dominions as a valiant and famous knight; and that even at this early period he was beginning to be enveloped in the mist of the unhistorical and the legendary.

3. Robert of Gloucester's Chronicle.

The first of the English works that comes under our notice is the metrical chronicle of Robert of Gloucester, which dates from about the year 1300. This is a history of England from the earliest period (beginning, according to the idea of those times, with the Trojan war) down to the year 1270, written in a very patriotic English spirit. For the first part of his Chronicle Robert drew principally from Geoffrey of Momnouth's Historia regum Britonum, in the introduction to the Chronicle and in that portion treating of the history of the Britons Henry of Huntingdon's Historia Anglorum and, to a less degree, William of Malmesbury's Gesta regum Anglorum being also used. For the Anglo-Saxon period the two last mentioned historians are the chief sources, and are drawn from to about an equal extent, while Henry of Huntingdon continues to be chiefly made use of up to the beginning of Henry II's reign. From that date on, the Waverley Annals supplied Robert with most of his material, besides which he used the Tewkesbury Annals and, probably, also Roger of Hoveden's chronicle.[24] Here and there Robert also introduces circumstances from his own personal experience, and occasional lines of his Chronicle are apparently not founded upon any of the works from which he is known to have taken material. The portion of the Chronicle that directly concerns us, that devoted to the reign of Richard I., consists of some 200 lines, which relate in a very prosaic style the course of events. Richard's coronation, the plundering of the Jews, the crusade, Richard's imprisonment on the homeward journey, his arrival in England, and his death are very

---

24) Further details as to the relation of Robert of Gloucester's Chronicle to the sources from which he drew are to be found in the articles by W. Ellmer in Anglia X, 1 ff. and 291 ff., Ueber die quellen der reimchronik Robert's von Gloucester. Compare also K. Brossmann's Ueber die quellen der mittelenglischen chronik des Robert von Gloucester, Breslau, Dissertation, 1887.

concisely sketched. In the midst of the account of events in the Holy Land the following interesting reference to a ‚romance' concerning Richard is to be found[25]:

„King richard bileuede þer   & so nobliche he wroȝte·
þat al þut lond þer aboute·   In is poer he broȝte·
Me nuste longe þer biuore·   neuer eft in heþenesse·
Of so noble kniȝt ne prince·   ne do so muche prowesse
Me ne mai noȝt al telle her·   ac wo so it wole iwite·
In romance of him imad·   me it may finde iwrite·

The ‚romance' here referred to by Robert of Gloucester is undoubtedly the metrical romance of Richard Coeur de Lion, which existed originally in French and was afterwards translated into English and in the course of time greatly enlarged beyond the compass of the original French version. Robert of Gloucester's reference to the romance is, as seen in the above 6 lines quoted from his Chronicle, of such a general kind that it is impossible from it alone to draw any conclusion as to the form in which he was acquainted with the romance — the French or the English.[26]

4. The Chronicle of Peter of Langtoft, and its translation by Robert Mannyng of Brunne.

Two other metrical chronicles may be conveniently considered together, namely, that in French alexandrines by Peter of Langtoft, a Canon of Bridlington in Yorkshire, and its translation into English by Robert Mannyng of Brunne (now Bourn) in Lincolnshire. The portion of these chronicles treating of the reign of Richard I. is much more expanded than the corresponding portion of that of Robert of Gloucester. As a historian, however, the latter is much more

---

25) W. Aldis Wright's ed., II. 694.

26) Ellmer's assertion, Anglia X, 294, „sicher ist jedenfalls, dass beide werke, das englische und das französische, einen und denselben inhalt gehabt haben" in only true in a general way. A considerable portion of the romance in its longest English form undoubtedly consists of additions made in English in England, which are not founded on any French original. See note 27.

accurate and independent than Langtoft or Mannyng, with both of whom the dividing line between legend and history is by no means sharply drawn. In his account of Richard's life and exploits Robert of Brunne offers many variations from, and additions to, his original; on the whole, however, his work is a fairly faithful reproduction of Langtoft.

It is not necessary here to follow in detail the course of the narrative as given by Peter of Langtoft and Robert of Brunne. From the king's coronation and his preparations for the crusade until his return to England the chronicles correspond, in their leading features and in the succession of events, to the facts of history. The sojourn of the king in Sicily, which is not at all mentioned by Robert of Gloucester, is here described with great minuteness.

In Langtoft, who wrote his Chronicle soon after the year 1307, and still more frequently in Robert of Brunne, whose translation was completed in 1338, we also meet with references to a „romance". Those made by Robert of Brunne are in many cases independent of Langtoft altogether, and show a direct acquaintance with the „romance" alluded to. It would lead too far afield to discuss here in which of its versions, the French or the English, this romance was known to Langtoft or to Robert of Brunne, or whether they knew both; but that the romance referred to by these writers in their chronicles is the metrical romance of Richard Coeur de Lion to be immediately taken into consideration, is evident from the references, amongst many others, in Robert of Brunne to the „mate Griffoun", Richard's engine of war used at Messina and Acres, to the tale of the archbishop of Pisa (here called „bisshop of Perouse"), to the battle of Caiphas, and to many other objects and events we shall presently meet with in a review of the romance itself.

5. The Metrical Romance and its different versions.

The figure of Richard, as he next meets us in English literature, is almost as much dimmed and altered by tradition as that of Charlemagne and his circle of peers. He has become an almost completely legendary personage, and much more fabulous than heroic. A long Metrical Romance with Richard as its hero, has been handed down to us. This extensive poem existed, as is evident, originally in a French form, and was afterwards translated and greatly added to by later English minstrels.[27]) The French original has, so far

---

27) That the groundwork of the romance of Richard Coeur de Lion was originally French is evident from the words of the English translator himself in numerous places. In the introduction to the poem we read (Weber ll. 21—24):

> In Frensshe bookys this rym is wrought,
> Lewede menne know it nought,
> Lewede menne cunne French non,
> Among an hondryd unnethis on.

Again (Weber 5059—5062):

> Off my tale be nowght a wundryd;
> The Frensche says he slowgh an hundryd
> (Wheroff is made this Ynglysche sawe),
> Or he reste hym ony thrawe.

Many more references to „the book", „tale", „story", „geste" are only different ways of pointing to the French original. In Weber's text these references are to be found in the following lines: 21—24, 37—42, 197—202, 1305—06, 1963—66, 2037—38, 2369—70, 2447—48, 2611—14 2873—79, 2953, 3415—16, 4847—4856, 5059—5062, 5277—78, 5358—60, 5625—30, 5710—11, 5812—13, 5840—41, 6153, 6433—36, 6487—88, 6543—44, 6947—50, 7039—41. Some of the lines here given may only be insertions on the part of the English poet to give an appearance of greater truthfulness or reality to his narrative, but the vast majority of them are genuine references to the French poem that he was rendering in English. That the English version grew in time to be much larger than the original French is also easily seen (1) from the lack of harmony between the different parts of the whole poem, which of itself would lead us to suppose interpolations; (2) from the absence of any reference whatever to a French original in large sections of the poem, which sections show in themselves a unity of plan, and are easily separable from what precedes them and from what follows; and (3) from the style of certain sections of the poem, which have an unmistakeably English flavour. The introduction (Weber 1—34) is of course English. Lines 35—240, in which is found the story of Cassodorien, contain references to „my sawe" and „the book", and thus probably formed part of the poem in its French form.

as is known, not been preserved, while the English form exists in several different versions, which will now be considered in succession.

a. The longest and most complete version is that preserved in a manuscript of Caius College, Cambridge, which was

---

In lines 240—1234 occur no references to an original of any kind whatever. The episode related in them, namely, Richard's tournament at Salisbury, his choice of Sir Thomas Multon and Sir Fulk Doyly as companions for the pilgrimage, the imprisonment in Almayn, the killing of the king of Almayn's son and of the lion, is evidently out of place here in the early part of the poem, because Richard never saw the Holy Land until he went there at the head of an army, as is told later in the poem. It is thus highly probable that this episode 240—1234 was later inserted here owing to the fact that the original French poem never contained the account of Richard's adventures in Almayn on his homeward journey, or that this portion of it, which would naturally form the close of the poem, had been lost or from some other cause remained unknown to the English poet. It is impossible to deny that this episode or a similar one may have been originally written concerning Richard in French, but, if so, it must be of later date than the main body of the French poem. And this lateness of origin, and especially the absence of references to any French original, point to its having been first written in English. — Another large section of the poem, Weber 4731—3788, is also to all appearance of English origin. It forms an episode complete in itself and only loosely connected with what goes before and what comes after; it is, as we shall see presently, not found in the Donce ms.; and is thoroughly English in spirit, as is seen from the lyric opening:

> Merye is, in the tyme of May,
> Whenne foulis synge in her lay;
> Floures on appyl trees, and perye;
> Smale foules synge merye, etc.

A minute examination of the relation between the romance in its various English forms and the French original is yet necessary, but lies outside the range of the present work. But from what is here pointed out it is plain that, though a French poem on Richard Coeur de Lion formed the groundwork of a corresponding English poem, this latter, even if at first a faithful reproduction of the French poem, has afterwards received in England large English additions which have no counterpart in the original French form.

printed in 1810 by Henry Weber.[28]) Of the contents of the poem as there found, the following is a synopsis.

ll. 1—24. Many romances are to be read of Roland and Oliver, Alexander and Charlemagne, Arthur, Gawain and other good knights; now I will tell you of Richard, who surpassed them all. This book is written in French; but unlearned men understand it not, for they know no French.
35—240. Story of Richard's birth. His father, king Henry, being persuaded by his barons to take to himself a wife, sends messengers to seek for the fairest woman that lives. At sea they meet a wonderful ship in which is Corbaryng king of Antioch, who, instructed in a vision, had set out with his daughter Cassodorien. The messengers conduct these two to king Henry, who weds Cassodorien. They had, as the book (i. e. the French original) says, two sons and a daughter — Richard, of whom this romance is made, John, and their sister Topyas. Cassodorien could not abide the elevation of the host at mass, and when the king consented that his knights should force her to remain in the church, she took her daughter and John, and flew aloft and out from the roof. John fell from the air and broke his thigh, while she and her daughter were never afterwards seen. King Henry at his death ordained Richard to be his successor.
241—1234. Richard is crowned in his 15th year, and grew to be a mighty and noble king. He held a tournament at Salisbury, to which he summoned all his knights in order to see who were the best among them. Richard during the course of the tournament disguises himself in three different attires, black, red and white. Sir Thomas Multon and Sir Fulk Doyly, who had proved themselves his bravest opponents, are afterwards summoned to the king's presence privately, and the latter chooses them to accompany him as

---

28) Metrical Romances Vol. II. Edinburgh, 1810.

palmers to the Holy Land. The three set out and pass through Flanders and many lands by way of Brandys (Brindisi) and Cyprus to the Holy Land, where they visit Acres, Babylon, Caesarea, Nineveh, Jerusalem, Jaffa and many other places. On their homeward journey they are in Almayn betrayed by a minstrel, whom they had not received in a friendly way, and fall into the hands of the king, who casts them into prison. Richard kills the king's son Ardour in a friendly exchange of buffets with the fist, in which case Richard used wax for his hand. The king's daughter Margery, who loves Richard, orders the gaoler to free the prisoner of his chains, and shows him all the courtesy of a fair lady of that chivalrous age. The king of Almayn takes counsel with his barons how he may avenge himself upon Richard for the death of his son. Sir Eldryd, the wisest of them, advises that, since it would be contrary to international laws of hospitality to hang a king, a savage lion be placed in prison with Richard. Margery warns the latter of the fate in store for him, but cannot prevail upon him to flee, as that would be against the law of the land. He stands in no fear of the lion, and promises Margery its heart by prime the third day; but asks her for silk kerchiefs to wind round his arm. That evening Margery provides a supper for Richard and his companions. After her departure on the following morning Richard winds the kerchiefs about his arm, and awaits the lion. When the beast was let into the prison Richard watched his chance and, thrusting his arm down the lion's throat, tore out the heart, lungs, liver and all else. Having returned thanks to God for his victory, he proceeds with the heart to the hall where the king sat at meat, and before the eyes of all he dips the heart into some salt and eats it — „withouten bred." From this feat he was afterwards called

    Kyng i-crystenyd off most renoun
    Stronge Rychard Coer de Lyoun.

The king of Almayn, who was then in great grief and rage for the death of his son and the disgrace of his daughter, ordains that a high ransom shall be the price of Richard's freedom.

> Off enny kyrk that preest in syng,
> Messe in sayd, or belle in ryng,
> There two chalyses inne bee,
> That on schal be brought to mee:
> And yiff there be moo than thoo,
> The halvyndel schal come me too.

Richard thereupon writes a letter to his chancellor in England, and in course of time the required amount is raised, and Richard set free. The king orders his daughter Margery to quit his land, but the queen, her mother, bids her wait until Richard shall send for her „as a kyng dos afftyr hys qwene." 1235—1420. Arrived in England, Richard and his companions receive a fitting welcome. After a year the king summons his Parliament to meet at London.

Before that time all the country of Bethlehem and the adjoining lands were in the hands of Christian men, and palmer and pilgrim might visit them without hindrance. The duke Mylon and earl Renaud held the land against the Sultan, until betrayed by the false earl Joys and Markes Feraut, when all the land of Syria and the holy cross were lost. „An holy Pope, that hyghte Urban" exhorted every Christian man to rise and avenge Jesus of his enemies; and many kings and princes, among them the king of France, the duke of Austria, the emperor of Almayn and others, responded to the call. King Richard, at a solemn feast held at Westminster, announces to his subjects his intention of also taking arms in the holy cause. Multitudes of his men assembled. He had 200 ships well victualled, and 13 ships laden with hives of bees; a strong tower of quaint device; and still another ship with an engine called Robynet. He sends on the ships in charge of his admiral Trenchemer to Marchyle (Marseilles), where they are to await his coming; for he will pass with a host through Almayn to call king Modard to account for having before detained him in prison.

1421—1658. Richard divides his host in three, allotting one portion to Sir Thomas Multon, another to Sir Fulk Doyly, and commanding the third himself. Before leaving England he appoints the bishop of York his chancellor, and commands the justices to rule aright and care for the poor. Having passed over sea and set out with his hosts for Coloyne (Cologne), Richard gives strict orders to take nothing from the inhabitants without paying for it. The people of the city refuse to sell fuel to Richard and his followers, whereupon the king orders his steward to buy up all the wooden vessels — dishes, cups, saucers, bowls, trays, platters, vats, tuns &c. — and with them prepare a meal. The poor people and the mayor of the city are also invited to partake of the feast. After further progress into the country, the king's daughter Margery comes to welcome Richard. Before the city of Marburette king Modard again seeks to impede their march by refusing them fuel. This time Richard evades the difficulty by ordering his steward to gather figs, raisins, nuts and all kinds of fruit, use some wax, tallow and grease along with these, and thereby make a fire. At the city of Carpentras king Modard casts himself at Richard's feet, but Margery intercedes for him, and the two kings are reconciled. Modard returns to Richard the money he had formerly extorted from him as ransom, and offers to join him in his crusade. This offer Richard will not accept owing to the king's great age, but receives two golden rings, the one of which will protect him from death by water, the other from death by fire. Richard then proceeds to Marseilles, where he finds his fleet waiting, and embarks for the Holy Land.

1659—3730. Arriving at Messina Richard finds king Philip of France already there. The latter endeavors in a treacherous way to turn Tancred, king of Poyle (Apulia), against Richard, but Tancred's son Roger, „kyng in Cesyle land" (Sicily), takes the part of Richard, and upon investigation the treasonable practices of Philip are laid bare.

At Christmas the enmity between the two kings' followers leads to serious conflict. In the city of Messina the French

and Griffons[29]) kill several Englishmen, whereupon Richard in anger captures the city by a land and sea attack, and after great slaughter brings the French to surrender. Richard's wonderfully constructed tower was from this event called Mate-Gryffon. Richard had pity for the king of France as he knelt to beg mercy,
    And light adown, so sayth the book,
    And in his armes up him took.
In March the king of France went on to Acres, and after Lent Richard followed. A storm threw some of his ships on the coast of Cyprus, and their crews were plundered by the islanders and cast into prison. When Richard came up three days later, he sent messengers to the emperor of Cyprus to demand the instant surrender of the prisoners. But the messengers met with a blunt refusal, and barely escaped from a knife the angry emperor threw after them, but which fortunately missed its mark and pierced a door. When the emperor's steward remonstrated with him for such treatment of a king's messengers, the emperor traitorously cut off his nose. Richard with his men lands upon the island, and with the assistance of the ill-treated steward is able to surprise the emperor's camp, where he secures much valuable booty, amongst it two noble steeds Favel and Lyarde, which he retains for his personal use. The emperor soon sues for mercy, which is granted him; but upon his proving traitorous to Richard again, the latter causes him to be bound and taken along into Syria.

 The earl of Leicester is left to govern Cyprus, while Richard proceeds to Acres. On the way thither the fleet falls in with, and captures, a ship laden with stores for the Saracens. Arrived at Acres, Richard stands on the prow of his ship and with his axe that was made of twenty pound of steel cleaves the chain drawn across the entrance to the harbor. The terrible engines of war he exhibits as the ships enter the harbor strike terror into the hearts of the Saracens.

---

29) Name commonly applied in the Middle Ages to the mixed inhabitants of Sicily.

Richard is received with great joy and honor by the king of France and the other Christian princes already there, and the archbishop of Pyse (Pisa) relates to him the sufferings of the Christians before his arrival. The siege, he said, had lasted seven years. On one occasion a noble steed had strayed away from one of the heathens, and 11,000 Christian knights, who sallied out to its capture, were slain. The Sultan also caused the water used by the Christians to be poisoned, resulting in the death of 40,000. On St. James eve the Saracens pretended to flee before the onset of the Christians, but after the latter had plundered their camp and were so impeded by the provisions and riches of all kinds they attempted to carry with them, the Saracens returned suddenly and slew 15,000 of the unprepared Christians. At Michaelmas 60,000 died of hunger. King Richard wept to hear this doleful tale, and begged the archbishop's prayers for his success. Commencing operations, he sets up his Mate-Gryffon, and also works great havock among the Saratens by the hives of bees he causes to be hurled into the city. He puts to flight a great host that had come to the assistance of the Saracens at Acres. In course of time Richard falls sick and longs for pork, which his steward is unable to procure. As a substitute, however, a portion of a Saracen prisoner is prepared and set before him. This, which he supposes all the while to be pork, he eats with great relish and recovers health. Later, when resting after battle, he calls for the head of that supposed swine. The steward with fear and trembling brings in the cooked head of the Saracen, but Richard is anything but wroth:

What devyl is this? the kyng cryde.
And gan to laughe as he wer wood.

He adds that so long as Saracens are to be had he and his followers need never want for food.

A proposal for peace, on the condition that Markes Feraunt be made king of Syria, is scornfully rejected by Richard. Acres surrenders, and the holy cross is given up. Messengers come from the Sultan to offer ransom for

the prisoners taken, when Richard terrifies them by setting
before them a meal prepared from the heads of their Saracen relatives, each with his name attached. Each of the messengers
>sat stylle, and pokyd othir,
They saide: This is the develys brothir
That sles our men and thus hem eetes.

Richard himself proceeds with the meal, and bids his guests be not „squoymous", as it was his custom as host.
>There is no flesch so noryssaunt,
Unto an Ynglysche man,
Patrick, plover, heroun, ne swan,
Cow ne oxe, scheep ne swyn,
As the hed off a Sarezyn.

Saladin then offers to give over Syria, Egypt and all the adjoining lands, if Richard will forsake Jesus and take Appolyn for lord. This offer is naturally refused, and when the Saracens say they do not know where the holy cross is, Richard orders 60,000 of the prisoners to be slain.

3731—4788. Richard holds a feast, and displays great liberality toward his followers, an example that is not followed by the king of France. A plan is arranged for the conquest of the whole country. Philip, more by vain display than by actual assault, brings the cities of Taburette and Archane to surrender, and, contrary to Richard's previous advice, takes ransom from the inhabitants.

Richard again divides his host into three parts, entrusting one to Sir Thomas Multon and one to Sir Fulk Doyly. With the third he himself subdues Sudan Turry (Sidon-Tyre) after a hard siege, and puts the citizens to the sword. Sir Thomas takes Castle Orglyous, and after the inhabitants had made an attempt to murder him and his men at might he shows no mercy; while Sir Fulk, upon defeating a great Saracen host on the plain before Ebedy, takes the city and treats the inhabitants in a similar manner. After these events the English and French assemble in Acres, and give account of their experiences. Philip is rebuked by Richard for having spared the towns of Taburette and Archane, and the two armies set out for these places again. The citizens, as was expected, deny entrance to Philip, whereupon they are subdued a second time and slaughtered; afterwards the two kings return to the sea-coast. 4789—7126. On his way to the city of Caiphas Richard is attacked by Saladin, but with great effort wards off the attack and puts the Sultan to flight. He repairs to the city of Palestyn and is forced to wait for provisions, while Saladin in the meantime levels many cities with the ground. Richard accepts the sultan's challenge to battle, and the two armies meet by the forest of Arsour. A noble knight, Jakes Denis, is killed, but his body recovered by Richard. The Turks are put to flight, and as Saladin flees from the field Richard sends an arrow after him which pierces his „shoulder bone". Richard and Philip besiege Nineveh. Three of the Saracen leaders challenge Richard, Sir Thomas and Sir Fulk to combat, which results in the death of all three heathens; whereupon the inhabitants of the city surrender. Richard calls a bishop to baptize them to the Christian faith.

Saladin flies to Babylon, where Richard and Philip besiege him. The latter traitorously accepts money from the Turks and desists from the siege. Saladin sends a challenge to Richard and at the same time the offer of a steed of great worth, which the latter accepts. A necromancer conjures two „fiends of the air" in the likeness of two steeds, mare and colt, the colt being sent to Richard, while the Sultan rides the mare. An angel warns Richard not to be afraid to ride the colt. Only an enormous lance forty feet long shall be fastened to the saddle and project out in front of the animal, the bridle shall be made fast upon its head. Its ears also are stopped with wax, Richard's axe and mace are strung to the saddle, and the other necessary preparations are made for the contest. On the morrow the two hosts meet, but before the contest is begun an oath is sworn that if Richard is victor all the Sultan's lands shall be handed over to him, while, in case the Sultan

wins, every Christian shall depart from the land. When the two leaders then dash towards each other, the Sultan's fiendish mare neighs loudly in order that, as the necromancer had ordained, the colt upon which Richard rode should run to its dame, and, as it knelt down, the Sultan should have his apponent at a disadvantage. Owing, however, to the wax in its ears, the fiendish colt hears nothing, and Richard, bearing down upon the Sultan with his huge tree-like lance, sends him
>Bakward ovyr hys meres croupe,
>The feet toward the fyrmament.
>Behynd the Sawdon the spere out went,

after which feat he dashes into the midst of the heathen host, working the greatest havoc wherever he goes
>For al that ever before hym stode,
>Hors and man, to erthe yode,
>Twenty foot on every syde.

Encouraged by his example, both English and French display the greatest valor, and ere long the town is taken. When the Sultan, who had only been wounded in the first encounter, sees that the men in the town have opened their gates he flees into a wood whither Richard is unable to follow him owing to the size of the tree-like lance, which demands so great a space for action.

After a sojourn of a fortnight there, Richard and Philip set out for Jerusalem. On the way thither a dispute arises between the two kings as to the ownership of Jerusalem after it shall have been taken. Philip grew sick for anger and, on the advice of his leech, returned to France, accompanied by the taunts of Richard. Thus their mutual enmity was increased,
>And aftyr that partyng, forsothe,
>Ever yitt they were wrothe.

Richard then repairs to Jaffa, which city he fortifies, and thence to Chaloyn (Ascalon) where he calls upon all the lords of the Christian host to assist in building up the walls. They all respond to the call except the duke of Austria who, when Richard courteously requests him to join in doing his share of the work, replies

> My fadyr n'as mason, ne carpentere;
> And though your walles should all to-schake,
> I schall nevir helpe hem to make.

At this Richard turns color with wrath, and maltreats the duke, ordering him to leave the host inside of three days.

> Traytour, we travayle day and nyght
> In werre, in wakyng, and in fyght,
> And thou lyes as a vyle glotoun,
> And restes in thy pavyloun,
> And drynkes the wyn good and strong,
> And slepes alle the nyght long.
> I schal breke thy banere
> And slynge it into the ryvere.

The duke departed after being thus insulted,

> And swore by Jesu in Trynyte,
> And he myghte ever hys tyme see,
> Off Richard sholde he be so awreke
> That al the worlde scholde theroff speke,

and the minstrel goes on to add that

> He heeld hym al to weel foreward:
> In helle myght he be hangyd hard.
> For, thorwgh hys tresoun and trehcherye,
> And thorwgh the waytyng off hys aspye
> Kyng Richard he dede gret schame,
> That turnyd all Yngeland to grame.
> A lytyl lenger had he most
> Have lyvyd, by the Holy Gost,
> Ovir king, duke, and emperour,
> He hadde ben lord and conqueror:
> Alle Crystyante, and al Paynym
> Scholde have holde under hym.

After the walls of Chaloyn are finished, the castles of Albary and Daroun are in succession taken, the latter with considerable difficulty. All prisoners except those who pay large ransoms are put to death. The engines of war, Mate-Gryffon and Robinet, are used with great effect at the siege.

Richard next distingiushes himself at the taking of Gatrys (Gaza, Gazara). The citizens had thrown open their gates upon a promise from Richard that their lives would be spared. In answer to his inquiry after the lord of the place Richard is told that a huge image set up in the centre of the city represents their lord, and the inhabitants agree to become Christians if Richard is able to break, as he proposes, the neck of the image by charging against it with his lance. Mounted upon his steed Favel of Cyprus, and armed with a mighty shaft, he severs the head of the image from the body, killing five Saracens underneath. When the old governor of Gatrys is brought before him, Richard generously hands over the city to him again. He returns to Chaloyn, and afterwards takes Leffunyde and the city of Gybelyn, which latter place the Knights of the Hospital and the Templars had held many a year.

Tidings now come from England of the treachery of his brother John, which Richard will not believe. At Bethany, which he next captures, other messengers arrive with similar tidings, and Richard is inclined to return privily to England to make peace with John, and return in haste to the Holy Land. At this juncture a Saracen enters with the news that an immense treasure is being taken to Saladin, and to tell Richard how he may capture it. The king refuses to take advantage of strategy against the large escort that has the treasure in charge, but defeats them openly and makes himself master of all their riches, which he distributes amongst his men.

Now come the bishop of Chester and the abbot of St. Alban with the news that John is about to have himself crowned king in England, and that the king of France has invaded Normandy. When Richard is at Acres about to depart for England, the Sultan, wishing to avenge the loss of his treasure, besieges the Christians in Jaffa. Henry of

Champagne is sent to their relief, but is unsuccessful. Enraged at this, Richard undertakes the task.

It was before the heygh myd nyght,
The moon and the sterres schon ful bryght,

as Richard with his galleys arrives at the city. All is quiet, until the dawn of day when Richard is comforted by learning that the beleaguered Christians are still holding out, through the reveille by which one of the watchmen announces the arrival of help. By the „time of evensong" the Saracens were driven from before the gates, and Richard that night made merry feasting with his men. The following day they are again attacked by a countless host of Saracens, but Richard, on his steed Favel, slaughters them by the hundreds. Multitudes are forced into a great mire outside Jaffa.

What ther wer drownyd, and what wer slawe,
The Sawdon loste off hethene lawe
Syxty thousand in lytyl stounde,
As it is in the Frensche i-founde.

Richard rescues his nephew Henry of Champagne from great peril, mowing the heathens down on his way.

Be the dymmyng off the more,
Men myghte see where Richard fore.

But the city is meanwhile again beset more violently than ever. Many prominent men among the Christians are slain before Richard makes his way to the gates. His steed Favel is slain under him, but on foot he slays two sons of Saladin and various other heathen leaders with his battle-axe. His other steed Lyard is brought.

Kyng Richard into the sadyl leap;
Then fledde the Sarezynes as they wer scheep.

On the morrow he sends messengers to the Sultan offering to fight single-handed five and twenty of his men, to decide thus the possession of the Holy Land. If this offer be not accepted, Richard asks a truce of three years, three months and three days, in order that he may return to England to arrange his affairs there, and come again. Saladin informs the messengers that he would not consent to a combat of even a hundred of his men against Richard, but is ready to make a truce. Christian men are then at liberty to wend their way to Jerusalem to the Sepulchre, and whithersoever else they will as pilgrims go.

> Kyng Richard, doughty off hand,
> Turnyd homward to Yngeland.
> Kyng Richard reynyd here
> No more but ten yere.
> Sythe he was schot, alas,
> In Castel-Gaylard ther he was.
> Thus endyd Richard our kyng:
> God geve us alle good endyng,
> And hys soule reste and roo,
> And oure soules whenne we com thertoo.
> Amen. Explicit.

b. The romance of Richard Coeur de Lion is preserved again in a ms. of the Bodleian Library in Oxford, in the collection Douce, No. 228. Many lines of the text are here lost. Those that are preserved correspond on the whole very closely with Weber, though many present variations as regards import, and many are also quite independent of, and complementary to, the text in Weber. The Douce ms. opens at l. 269 of Weber.

> Kyng Re cam̄ owt of a valey. (edge torn)
> ffor to fulfellyn þᵉ knyhts pl . . .
> As a knyth þᵗ wer aventor . . .
> His atyr was orgilous
> Altogedʳ col blac
> Wᵗ owtyn̄ ony kyngys lac
> Upon his crest a ravyn stod
> þᵗ g . . . yd as he hadde be wod
> Abowte his nekke hynge a bell
> A reson by I schal ȝow tell

It then proceeds with the account of the tournament at Salisbury, which is shorter than in Weber; of the journey to Palestine in company with Sir Thomas Multon and Sir Fulk Doyly; and of the imprisonment on their return. The lion exploit differs considerably from the account in Weber. Richard, upon refusing to flee with the king's daughter Margeryte, begs of her not only the silken kerehiefs but also a knife:

> Do me to haue kerchis of sylke
> A doseyn iwyth as ony mylke
> & a long Irysch knyf
> As þᵘ wilt saue my lyf

Richard and his two companions are treated in the same hospitable way by Margeryte that evening, and on the following morning the lion is led into the prison, „a wyld best þᵗ was sauage."

> & kyng Ricʳ also sket
> In þᵉ lyonnys throte his harm he schet
> Al in kerchis his harm was wonde
> The lyon he strangelyd on a stoñde
> Wᵗ his pawys his kertil he rof
> Wᵗ þᵉ lyon to þᵉ erthe he drof
> Ricʳ wᵗ þᵉ knyf so smert
> strok þᵉ lyon to þᵉ hert
> Owt of his kerchis his harm he drow
> At þᵗ gamyn Ricʳ low
> & þᵉ kerchis still he lette
> þus þᵉ lyon wᵗ his macche mette
> He hopenyd hym at þᵉ brest boñ
> & tok owt his herte a noñ
> And thankyd god omnipotent
> Of þᵉ grace he hadde hym sent
> & for þis dede of gret renoñ
> He was i callyd queor delyoñ

After a time the king sends some knights to the prison who, contrary to their expectations, find Richard unharmed with the lion dead beside him. The king exacts as ransom gold and silver enough „an house to ffill". When the money had been collected and Richard is leaving the country he vows vengeance.

> Kyng Ricʳ swor be seynt Johñ
> That he wolde haue too for on

a threat, however, which he does not carry out, for, strange to say, ll. 1238—1658 of Weber have no parallel here. Only 24 lines tell of his return to England and the preparations for the crusade. The second visit to Almayn is entirely omitted, Richard with his host going directly to Marseilles, and thence to Messina. The events in Sicily correspond closely, though the following noteworthy lines based upon actual history occur, in the place of Weber 2027—2032.

> Kyng Ricʳ sesyd & rest
> ffro cristemesse þᵗ heye ffest
> And dwellyd a tul ageyne þe lente
> His modʳ hī brout a fayr pʳsent
> Elyanor brouȝt hī Berynger
> The kyngs dowtʳ of Naȝer
> Kyng Rogʳis wyf cā wᵗ her than
> . . . . . . sche hythe a ffayr womañ
> Kyng Ricʳ þᵉ pʳcyous
> Beryngʳ he schuld spouse
> E seyde he nold not in swylk seson
> spouse her among þᵉ Grefoñ
> He wolde her spouse to be his wif
> Elianor her leue tok
> & went fforth so seth þⁱᵉ bok
> In marche monyth þᵉ kyng of fʳns
> Dede hym to chip wᵗ owtyn distᵘns

The ms. continues parallel to Weber through the events in Cyprus, the capture of the treasure-ship on the way to Acres, the tale of the archbishop of Pisa, and the operations commenced by Richard. The cure by Saracen's flesh offered instead of pork, as related in Weber 3019—3102, and also the subsequent fabulous accounts of the devouring of the

Saracens by Richard in ll. 3163—3202 and ll. 3323—3672, have no parallel here.

The offer of Saladin to make Richard king of the countries about the Holy Land if he should renounce the Christian faith, and Richard's subsequent order for the beheading of the prisoners at Acres correspond. Lines 3731—4788 of Weber, which contain the account of the taking of Taburet and Archane by king Philip, of Sudan Turry by Richard, of castle Orglyous by Sir Thomas, of Ebedy by Sir Fulk, and of the retaking of Taburet and Archane by the combined hosts, are here unrepresented. Next follows the attack by Saladin upon Richard on the way to Caiphas, and the death of Jakes Denis in the battle by the forest of Arsour, corresponding almost line for line with Weber 4789—5146. The account of the siege of Nineveh, the Sultan's stratagem to take Richard by means of the conjured horse at the siege of Babylon, and the later quarrel between Richard and Philip on the way to Jerusalem, as given in Weber 5147—5888, are not found here. Richard fortifies Jaffa, as in Weber 5889—5900. Between ll. 5900 and 5901 occurs the following historical reference.

> þͬ inne he dede beringer
> his quen þᵗ was his lef & der
> And Jhone his sustͬ þᵗ was a quene
> ffor þᵉʸ schulde at ese bene

Again, between lines corresponding to Weber 5908 and 5909, we find the following:

> To Torye he went be Brem
> ffour myle from Jerlm̄
> Tho haddyn þᵉ cristen gret blysse
> ffor þᵉⁱ wendyn wel I wisse
> þᵉⁱ schuldyn on morow h͡ oward in her Jurne
> qwanne þᵉⁱ haddyn woñy͡ Jerlm̄ Cete
> & so þᵉⁱ haddy͡ wᵗ owtyn fayll
> Ne . . . . hadde be Gautͬis coñsayll
> Gautͬ naþeles þᵉ ospiteler

  þer was he no good cõnseler
  Anon wt owtyn lesyng
  Thus he seyde to our kyng
  Ricr yf þu Jerlm̃ wynne
  þrow þy cowytyse & þy gŷne
  þy folke schal þe stede a nõn
  That god was onne to deth dõn
  & qwanne þei hau dõn her viage
  And holy al her pilgrimage
  heye & lowe squier E grom
  Hastely wyl heym hom
  Turne ʒou õn syde toward chaloyne
  That weye ys toward babiloyne
  & draw ʒou ford in to paynyme
  Wel ʒe schul be settyn ʒour tyme
  And saladyn þe soudõn
  ʒe schul hI þr quik tan
  To his consel þe kyng lyst
  þof yt wer not þe best
  Many Erl & baroun forsoþe
  ffor þt tydyng þei wer ful wroþe
  & wenty͡ hom in to her c͡ntr
  And let Ricr þre still be

Richard's quarrel with the duke of Austria at the building of the walls of Chaloyn, as told in Weber 5909—5996, is also found here. Of the taking of Albary and Daroun, Weber 5997—6164, however, nothing is said. Next follow the taking of Gatrys, and Richard's ˙breaking down of the image; the return to Chaloyn and the taking off Leffunyde and Gybelyn; the arrival of messengers from England, and the other events in regular succession up to the beginning of the siege of Jaffa by Saladin, — the whole corresponding almost line for line with Weber 6165—6590. Here, at the foot of a leaf which is badly torn, the ms. Douce 228 ends.

  c. In the ms. of the British Museum catalogued as Additional 31,042, a third version of the romance is preserved. Several folia of this ms. have been lost, and others are much

mutilated, but these constitute a very small proportion of
the whole, and from those that still exist intact we may
reasonably infer that, as far as the course and import of
the narrative is concerned, the version here given corresponded
exactly with that of Weber. Hardly any two lines of the
two texts, however, agree word for word, those of the ms.
now under consideration being almost invariably expanded;
in which process they have lost much of the grace and
lightness of the octosyllabic lines of the romance as it
exists in the ms. printed by Weber. It would appear that
the ms. Additional 31,042 is the work of some scribe devoid
of fine poetic sense, who in the attempt to make the lines
more explicit in their meaning, has shorn them of what
charm they possessed. That the writer of this ms. at all
events did not confine himself to reproducing accurately the
copy before him is clear from a mistake he made in one
place of writing a second time twenty lines which had a
place in a earlier part of the narrative, and which, after
discovering his mistake, he drew his pen through. The
writing shows plainly that both versions are the work of the
same scribe, so that it is interesting to compare them. The
lines refer to the deliberations between the king of Almayn
and his knights as to the most expedient way of disposing
of Richard, and in their proper place in the narrative read
as follows.

    And thus þan ansuerde þay þᵉ kynge
    Wᵗ owttyn any oþʳ lesyng
    Bot a knyghte þan spak vn to þᵉ kyng
    And seid hym Sir grefe the na thyng
    ffor Sir Eldrede for sothe y wysse
    He kañ telle the here of whate beste es
    ffor he es a wonder wyse mañ of rede
    And many a mañ hase he demyde to dede
    The Kyng comande þañ wᵗ owtteñ lett
    þat he were swythe by fore hym fett
    þan was he broghte by fore þᵉ kynge
    þat asked hym sone wᵗ owtteñ lesynge

> And seid kane yᵘ me telle in any manere
> How one Kyng Richerd þᵗ I vengid were
> And he ansuerde wᵗ hert full fre
> And seid þʳ appoñ I muste avyse me
> ffor ȝe wote wele it es no lawe
> A Kynge to hange nor ȝit to drawe
> Bot ȝe schall done by my resoune
> Hastyly takes ȝoʳ grete lyoune

In the middle of the archbishop of Pisa's tale where the scribe inadvertently inserted them again, these lines are given thus:

> And thus they ansuerde vn to þᵉ kyng
> With owtteñ any lesynge
> Bot þañ a knyghte spake vnto þᵉ kynge
> Sir he seid grefe the no thyng
> Sir Eldrede for sothe I wysse
> He cañ wele telle what beste es
> ffor he es wyse & gude of rede
> ffull many a mañ has he demyde to dede
> The kynge comande thane wᵗ owtteñ lett
> Swythe þᵗ he were by fore hym fett
> He was broghte by fore the kyng
> That askede hym sone wᵗ owte lesynge
> Kane you me telle one any manere
> Of this Kyng Richerde þᵗ I vengede were
> And he ansuerde wᵗ herte full fre
> There appoñ me moste avyssede be
> ȝee wote full wele it es no lawe
> A Kyng noþʳ to hange ne to drawe
> Bot ȝe schall done be my resoune
> Hastely takes ȝoʳ grete lyoune

The lines of this version of the romance that are missing owing to the loss of portions of the ms. are those corresponding to Weber 3087—3588, 4949—5034 and 6316—6604. The following extracts, together with those given above, will suffice to furnish an idea of the style of the whole. The ms. opens thus:

Lorde Jhū Criste kyng of glory
þe faire grace and the victorye
þat thou sent to kynge Richerde
þat neuͬ in his lyue was funden cowerde
It is righte gude to heryn in ieste
Off his prowesche and his noble conqueste
Also full fele romance men make newe
Of gude knyghtis þt were stronge & trewe
Of þaire dedis men redys Romance
Bothe iñ yglonde and eke iñ ffraunce
Of Duke Rowlande and of Sir Olyuere
And also of euͬe ylke a duzzepere
Of Alexandere and of Sir Gawayne
Of kyng Arthure & of Sir Charlemayne
How they weren gude and also curtayse
Of Bischope Turpyn & Sir Ogere Danays
And also of Troye men redis iñ Ryme
Whate werre was there ī olde tyme
Of Ectoure and also of Achilles
And whate folkes were slayne þͬ ı þᵗ prese
In ffraunce Bokes thies rymes men wrote
Bot in Ynglys lewede men knewe it note
Lewede men kan ffraunce righte none
Amanges ane hundrethe vnnethes one
Bot nowe will I schewe ȝow wᵗ gude chere
ȝiff that ȝow lyke to lythe & here
A noble geste I undirstonde
Off doughty knyghtis of Iglonde
And ther fore nowe I will ȝow rede
Of a Kyng that was doughty in dede
Kyng Richerde þᵗ was þᵉ werryoure beste
þat men redes offe in any geste
And to alle þat heris þ's ilke talkynge
Jhū now graunte theym his dere blyssynge

The lines in Weber 6657—6674, containing reference to the other well-known romances, read in the present version as follows:

Bot nowe herkyns my tale for it es sothe
þof þᵗ I swere ȝow þʳ to none othe
I will ȝow nenen romance none
Of Partynope ne of Charlemayne
Of Kyng Arthoure ne of Sir Gawayne
Ne ȝitt of Sir Launcelott de lake
Of Beues ne of Sir Gy ne of Sirake (?)
Nor of Uly nor ȝitt Sir Octouayne
Nor ȝitt of Sir Ectore the strange man
Of Jasone ne ȝitt of Ercules
Of Eneas ne ȝitt of Achilles
ffor I ne wene neuʳ per ma faye
þat in the tyme of their daye
Did any of theym so many doughty dede
Nor ȝitt so strange Batell in þaire nede
Als Kyng Richerde dide Saunce fayle
Att Jaffe in this ilke Bataylle

The concluding lines of the romance, corresponding to Weber 7119 ff., are as follows: —

And than aftir warde alle these thre ȝere
Cristyn men bothe fferre and nere
ȝode the wayes to Jerusalem
To the holy Sepulcre & to Bedelem
And to alle othir pilgremage
With owtten harme or any damage
And kyng Richerde þᵗ was doughty of hande
Torned hamwarde in to Ynglande
Kyng Richerde regned here
Noghte bot allanly ten ȝere
Sythyn was he slayne wᵗ schotte allas
At the castelle Galyarde there he was
And thus Endys þᵉ Romaunce of Richerd oure Kynge
And god grante vs alle gude Endynge amen
    Explicit The Romance
    Of Kyng Richerd þᵉ Cōqueroure

d. A portion of the romance is preserved again in the British Museum ms. Harley 4690, consisting of 1608 lines. This version, so far as it goes, agrees closely with that offered by the ms. Douce 228 already described. In a few places slight variations occur, and a few lines in ms. Douce 228 have no parallel here.

The opening lines describe the close of the tournament at Salisbury and Richard's contest with „Syr ffoukedoly", in which, contrary to the version given in Weber, the latter is unhorsed. Sir Thomas and Sir Fulk are summoned by the king, who informs them of his intention to visit the Holy Land, before he reveals himself as the knight who had so distinguished himself at the tournament. The account of the adventures in Almayn agrees in all respects with the ms. Douce 228, where both of these versions offer variations from Weber. Mention is also made here of the Irish knife.

 Do me to have kerchewes of sylke
 ffourty wyte as any mylke
 and a scherpe yrysche knyfe
 As þ^u wilte saue my lyfe.

The following lines describing Richard's victory over the lion, will also serve to show the close connection between this version and that of ms. Douce 228.

 And Kyng Richard also skette
 Yn to ys throte ys arme he schette
 Alle ynne kerchewes ys arme wownd
 the lyoune he strangled in þ^t stownd
 Richarde w^t the knyfe so smerte
 Smote the lyon to the herte
 Atte þatt game Richarde lowghe
 And of ys harme þe kerchewes drowe.
 He openedde hym atte þe breste bone
 And touke oute ys herte anone.
 And thonked godde omnipotente
 Of the grace he hadde hym sente
 And of this dede of grete renowne
 cleped he was conquer de lyoune.

The narrative then runs parallel with Douce until the return to England, with the exception that nothing is said of any intercession of the queen for her daughter, thus leaving us to suppose that the latter accompanied Richard on his departure from Almayn.

> Kyng Richard swere by seint Joon
> He wolde haue too for oon
> thanne the kyng. y vnderstonde
> towke ys dowghter by the honde
> and bad her wyth Richarde goo
> Oute of ys londe for euer moo
> He swore by alle ys parage
> thare schuld sche have non herytage
> thws come Richarde owte of pryson
> God ʒeffe vs alle ys Benesoune.

The second visit to Almayn is here also entirely omitted, and the preparations for the crusade are told even more concisely than in Douce; after which the two mss. run closely parallel to the end of this fragment, which closes in the middle of the archbishop of Pisa's tale with the line

> On a Seynt James day veramente,

corresponding to Weber 2755.

e. The celebrated Auchinleck ms. in the Advocates' Library at Edinburgh preserves still another fragment of 340 lines of the romance, which agree for the most part very closely with the version printed by Weber. It is curious to note that the opening 24 lines have been transformed into two of the 12-line stanzas familiar in later romances such as Amis and Amiloun and Sir Amadas, after which the ms proceeds in the usual octosyllabic couplets.

> Lord Jhesu king of glorie
> Swiche auentour and swiche victorie
> Thou sentest king Richard
> Min it is to leren his stori
> And of him to haue in memorie
> That neuer no was couward
> Bokes men maketh in latyn
> Clerkes witen what is ther in

> Bothe Almaundes and Pikard
> Romaunce make folk of Fraunce
> Of knichtes that wer in destaunce
> That dyed thurth dint of sward
> Of Rouland and of Oliuer
> And of the other duke Per
> Of Alisaunder and Charlemeyn
> Hector the gret werrer
> And of Danys lelich (?) Oger
> Of Arthur and of Gaweyne
> Ac this romaunce of frenys [is wroucht]
> That mani lewed no knowe noucht
> In gest aslo (?) we seyn
> This lewed no can freyns non
> Among an hundred unneth on
> On lede is noucht to leyn

The ms. then continues: —

> No the les with gode chere
> Fele of hem wald y here
> noble gestes ich vnderstond
> Of deukes knichtes of Inglond
> Ther fore now ich il ȝou rede
> Of a knicht douhti of dede
> King Richard the werrour best
> That men findeth in ani gest
> Thon al that listen this aming
> Jhesu hem grant gode ending

After this introduction there evidently occurs a break in the copy, for the lines immediately following correspond to those in Weber 1303 ff.

> A freyns knicht the douke Miloun
> Douke Renaud a bold baroun
> Thurth tresoun of the counte Roys
> Surri was lorn and the holy croys
> The douke Renaud was hewen smale
> Al to peces so seys the tale

The second visit to Almayn is here also omitted, Richard going direct to Marseilles, and thence to Messina. The account of events there agrees line for line with Weber, as far as their import is concerned, though in every case presenting variations in language, from l. 1659 to 1744. Here a great break occurs, owing to several leaves being lost, and Weber 1745—2762, containing the account of the quarrels in Sicily, of the events in Cyprus, the capture of the treasure-ship, and the arrival at Acres, have no parallel in this fragment. The next lines belong to the middle of the tale of the archbishop of Pisa, corresponding to Weber 2763 ff.

> Thai seyche the Sarraʒins had riches
> And we of all gode destresse
> And thoucht winne to her preye
> Of that tresour and that nobleye

From here to the close of the archbishop's story, and through the account of Richard's preliminary operations against Acres with his Mate-Gryffon, robinet, and the bee-hives, the ms. runs line for line parallel to Weber from l. 2763 to l. 2936, where it ends as follows: —

> That day so Richard sped ther
> That he was holden conquerer
> For better he sped that day ar none
> Than the other in seuen ʒer hadde done.[31])

f. In the Bodleian Library is also an interesting blackletter copy of the romance, printed by Wynkyn de Worde in the year 1528. Each section into which the poem is here divided is headed by a wood-cut representing the chief event described in the narrative that follows. As to content, however, this edition offers little that is new, as it is only a modernized form of the version given in Weber and, allowing for the

---

31) This fragment in the Anchinleck ms. was copied for me by the courtesy of a friend, so that I cannot, as in the case of the other mss., personally vouch for the accuracy of every letter.

difference in language and in variations as to words and phrases, agrees line for line with Weber from beginning to end, with the exception that lines 5147—5340 of Weber, in which is contained the account of the siege of Nineveh and of the combat with the three Saracen leaders, have no counterpart here, and that the closing lines of this black-letter copy have been expanded, as will be seen. It is not the case, as Weber asserts in the introduction to his edition, that „the savage meal which Richard made upon the heads of the Saracens, and the feast he prepared for the messengers of Soliman, are here omitted." These lines, and those concerning Richard's longing for pork, are found in Wynkyn de Worde's printed copy exactly parallel with Weber.[82]) I will give the following passages to show the general relation existing between the two texts. Wynkyn de Worde's copy opens as follows: —

  Lorde kynge of glorye
  Such grace and such . . . . [torn]
  Thou sendest to kyng . . . . . .
  That neuer was foun . . . .
  It is good to here Je . . . . .
  Of his prowesse and his conquestes
  Many romances men make newe
  Of good knyghtes and of trewe
  Of theyr dedes men rede romauns
  Bothe in Englonde and in Fraunce
  Of Rowlande and of Olyvere
  And of euery desepere
  Of Alysaunder and of Charlemayne
  Of kynge Arthur and of Gawayne
  How they were knyghtes good and curtoys
  Of Turpyn and of Oger the danoys
  Of troye men rede in ryme

---

  82) But it would be a laborious task to enumerate all the instances in which Weber and his contemporaries seem to have drawn upon their imagination instead of looking up the facts.

What was by olde tyme
Of Hector and of Achylles
What folke they slewe in prees
In fraunce these rymes were wrought
Euery englysshe ne knewe it nought
Lewde man cun frensshe none
Of an hondred unneth one
Neuertheles with gladde chere
Yff that ye wyll now here
Newe Jestes I vnderstonde
Of doughty knyghtes of Englonde
Therfore now I wyll you rede
Of a kynge doughty of dede
Kynge Rycharde was the beste
That is founde in ony Jeste
Now all that here this talkynge
God gyue them good endynge

Weber 6657 ff. are here: —

Herken now how my tale goth
Though I swere to you no othe
I wyll you rede romaynes none
Of Pertonape ne of Ypomydone
Ne of Alysaunder ne of Charlemayne
Ne of Arthur ne of Gawayne
Ne of Launcelot de lake
Ne of Beuys ne Guy of Sydrake
Ne of Ury ne of Octauyan
Ne of Hector the stronge man
Ne of Jason neyther of Achylles
They ne wanne neuer parmafaye
In thyr tyme by theyr daye
And anone of them so doughty dede
Ne so stronge batyll ne of felowrede
As dyde kynge Rycharde without fayle
At Jaffe at that stronge batayle

The closing lines of this version give the „duke of Estryche"
as being with his host in „castell Gaylarde" when Richard

was wounded by one of the defenders from the walls. For the sake of the further historical reference to Richard's burial, I will reprint these lines here[33]), which take the place of the closing ten lines in Weber:

 Thus Kyng Rychard that doughty man
 Peas made with the Sowdan
 And sith he came I vnderstonde
 The waye to warde Englonde
 And thorugh treason was schotte alas
 At castell Gaylarde there he was
 The duke of Estryche in the castell
 With his hoost was dyght full well
 Rycharde thought there to abyde
 The weder was hote in somer tyde
 At Gaylarde vnder the castell
 He wende he myght haue keled hym well
 His helme he abated thare
 And made his vysage all bare
 A spye there was in the castell
 That espyed Rycharde ryght well
 And toke an arblaste swythe stronge
 And a quarell that was well longe
 And smote Kynge Rycharde in tene
 In the heed without wene
 Rycharde let his helme downe fall
 And badde his men dyght them all
 And swore by the see and the sonne
 Tyll the castell were iwonne
 Ne sholde neyther mete ne drynke
 Neuer into his body synke
 He set up Robynet that tyde
 Upon the castelles syde
 On that other halfe the one
 He set up the matgryffone

---

33) They are also to be found in Weber II, 476.

To the castell he threwe stones
And brake the walles for the nones
And so within a lytell tyde
Into the castell they gan ryde
And slewe before and behynde
All tho that they myght ayenst them fynde
And euer was the quarell by the lede
Stycked styll in Rychardes hede
And whan it was drawen out
He dyed sone withoute doute
And he commaunded in al thynge
To his fader men sholde hym brynge
That they ne let for nesshe ne harde
Tyll he were at the forte Euerarde[34])
At fort Euerarte wytterly
His bones lye his fader by
Kynge Harry forsothe he hyght
All Englonde he helde to ryght
Kynge Rycharde was a conquerour
God gyve his soule moche honour
No more of hym in Englysshe is wrought
But Jesu that us dere bought
Graunte his soule reste and ro
And ours whan it cometh therto
And that it may so be
Say all amen for charyte.

Here ends the list of versions of the romance of Richard Coeur de Lion with which I am directly acquainted. Another ms. of it is preserved in the library of the College of Arms. This, according to the description given by Hardy in his „Descriptive Catalogue of Materials relating to the History of Gt. Britain and Ireland"[35]), contains the account of Richard's pilgrimage, his exploits in Germany, return to Germany with his host, and the events in the Holy Land, ending with Richard's return.

---

34) King Henry II., Richard's father, was buried at Fontevrault.
35) Vol. II, 519. See also Ellmer, Anglia X, 294f.

A fragment of the romance is also to be found in a ms. in the possession of the Marquis of Stafford, commencing with Richard's arrival at Messina, and ending with the truce with Saladin.[36])

Taking a final glance back at what has here been said concerning these 6 different texts of the romance, we see that they all point to one and the same original. The four longer texts, Weber (W), Douce 228 (D), British Museum Additional 31,042 and Wynkyn de Worde's black-letter copy, differ slightly here and there in the matter treated of, but for the great bulk of the poem agree very closely. The fragment, Harley 4690, is more closely connected with D than with the others, while the smaller Auchinleck fragment, with the exception of the first 24 lines in stanza form, shows most affinity with W. Where one or other of these English texts presents divergence in point of matter from one or more of the others, it is almost certain that this particular part of the text is of purely English origin, and a later addition to the translation from the French. Such is the case with the lines treating of Richard's cure by pork, and his fabulous devouring of Saracens (Weber 3019— 3102, 3163—3202 and 3323—3672), which are not found in D at all. By eliminating all such later additions and interpolations, there would be left the substance of an English poem forming the bulk of these six texts, and which poem would probably be a pretty faithful reproduction of the original romance in French concerning Richard Coeur de Lion. This original French poem plainly followed the facts of history more closely, and was freer from fabulous extravagances than the later English versions. It also either ended with Richard's departure from Palestine and did not contain an account of his imprisonment in Germany, or else the closing portion of it was unknown to the first English translator.

---

36) See Hardy II, 520. The extracts given by Hardy from the romance are not to be relied upon for literal accuracy.

IV.
Later Works in chronological Order.

From the early part of the fourteenth century until the close of the sixteenth Richard Coeur de Lion seems to have disappeared from among the notables who formed the subject of song or story, and his name, like that of so many of the heroes of the Middle Ages who had in the course of time developed into monstrosities of knighthood, was preserved only in the compilations of the chroniclers. When he appears again in literature it is in a different rôle. Many of the legends that were early connected with his name have come to be looked upon as actual facts of history, but from now on he is no longer the performer of fabulous feats of strength and skill, but is treated seriously as a historical personage of the past. These later works in which he appears again will now be taken up in chronological order.

1. The Troublesome Raigne of John King of England, with the discouerie of King Richard Gordelions Base Sonne etc.

This play printed in 1591 is the basis of Shakespeare's King John. We read on the title-page that „it was (sundry times) publikely acted by the Queenes Maiesties Players, in the honourable Cite of London", and was thus amongst the many plays which our great dramatist found attracting large audiences there, and which he considered worthy of remodelling.

Here, as in the closing lines of the romance quoted above from Wynkyn de Worde's printed copy, the duke of Austria is the cause of Richard's death. A further step is made in the union of the duke of Austria and the viscount

of Limoges (possessor of the castle of Chaluz where Richard met his death) in one person. Philip Fawconbridge, Richard's bastard son, avenges the death of his father by killing this representative of two historical names. The king of France, who is supporting the claims of the young Arthur to the throne of England, as prior to those of king John, says
„Braue Austria cause of Cordelion's death
Is also come to aide thee (Arthur) in thy warres."
and Lymoges adds vauntingly upon this reference to himself:
„Me thinkes that Richard's pride and Richard's fall
Should be a president t'affright you all."
The Bastard, in a battle that takes place, pursues Lymoges, depriving him of the lion's skin which he had previously taken from Richard, and later accomplishes his revenge in the death of his father's enemy; upon which follows this monologue with an allusion to Richard's rough treatment of the duke of Austria in Palestine: —
„Bastard. And as my father triumpht in thy spoyles
And trode these Ensignes vnderneath his feete,
So doo I tread vpon thy cursed selfe,
And leaue thy bodie to the fowles for food"

The reference contained in these lines, and especially the uniting of the duke of Austria and the viscount of Limoges in one person, seem to indicate that the author of this play of The Troublesome Raigne of John was acquainted with the romance of Richard as contained in the version printed by Wynkyn de Worde in 1528.

Shakespeare, in his allusions to Richard in the play of King John, simply follows the old play. The Bastard, when told by his mother that he is really Coeur de Lion's son, exclaims (Act I. Sc. 1).
„Your fault was not your folly;
Needs must you lay your heart at his dispose, —
Subjected tribute to commanding love, —
Against whose fury and unmatched force
The awless lion could not wage the fight,

Nor keep his princely heart from Richard's hand.
 He, that perforce robs lions of their hearts,
 May easily win a woman's."

Again (Act II. Sc. 1).

„Lewis (the Dauphin). Before Angiers well met, brave Austria.
Arthur, that great fore-runner of thy blood,
Richard, that robbed the lion of his heart,
And fought the holy wars in Palestine,
By this brave duke came early to his grave.

. . . .

Arthur. God shall forgive you Coeur de Lion's death,
The rather, that you give his offspring life."

By Shakespeare, in conformity with the old play, the duke of Austria and the viscount of Limoges are also made one and the same person, upon whom the Bastard avenges Richard's death.

2. The Tragedy of Richard I. King of England, To which are annexed Some other Papers. By George Sewell, M. D., late of Hampstead, all faithfully published from his original Manuscripts, by his Brother. London 1728.

This is a portion of an unfinished play founded on the life of Richard. The dedication is interesting from its reference to the approval of the subject of the play by Addison.

„To his Grace the Duke of Newcastle.

My Lord,

The opera of Richard the First being the present entertainment of the court, and my brother having signified to your Grace, that he was honoured with the sentiments of Mr. Secretary Addison, in thinking this a proper subject for the Drama, drew some scenes in order to the forming a tragedy thereon. In the address to your Lordship prefixed to the last collection of his poems, printed in the year 1820, he first applies to Mr. Addison, and concludes his apostrophe to your Grace in the following lines.

O! had you liv'd to fan the kindled rage,
E'en I the least, the lowest of the stage
To your own fav'rite them the lyre had strung,
And great Plantagenet triumphant sung,
First of his line, which mighty in extent
Shines forth in George, and brightens by descent.
Then had you heard the poet-monarch's strains
And view'd your Garter first on Jewry's Plains.

Upon this motive, my Lord, I hope you will forgwe the present interruption, since I look upon it as my incumbent duty to put these papers of my brother's under your protection, being, with most profound respect.
   Your Grace's Obedient
     Humble Servant.
       Gregory Sewell."

Preceding the tragedy itself is a history of the life of Richard. The unfinished play consists merely of three scenes of Act I., one scene of Act II., and a few other scattered scenes unnumbered. The last scene shows Richard on a conch in his tent wounded. He dies in commonplace philosophisings upon life and death.

From these few scenes that we have, there is no great cause for regret that the play remained a fragment.

3. Richard Coeur de Lion, comédie en trois actes, melée d'ariettes. Par M. J. Sedaine.[37]

This comedy, interspersed with music, was performed for the first time at Paris in October 1784 and, from the numerous imitations it called forth, seems to have enjoyed considerable popularity. It is founded upon the fiction of the discovery of Richard's place of imprisonment in the castle of Linz by the minstrel Blondel.

---

[37] M. J. Sedaine 1719—1797. His vaudevilles and operettas attracted the attention of Diderot. Two of his plays, which were very original and free from the prevailing excessive sentimentality, were performed at the Théâtre Français. Sedaine was later elected member of the Academy.

Act I. Florestan, the governor of the castle, is in love with Laurette, the daughter of Sir Williams, an exiled English knight living near by. Blondel, feigning blindness, is led by the youth Antonio to the vicinity of the castle. A letter sent by Laurette to the governor is intercepted by her father, and Blondel learns its contents. Marguerite, countess of Flanders and Artois, who has long been desolate owing to the imprisonment of her lover Richard, arrives at the house of Sir Williams and, on hearing a familiar air played by Blondel, calls the latter to her presence.

Act II. At dawn next day Blondel plays before the castle walls and is answered by Richard who sings to the same melody, the master and faithful adherent thus recognizing each other. Soldiers arrest Blondel for disturbance but, upon being brought before the governor, he wins favor with the latter by imparting to him the message from Laurette, and is set free again.

Act III. Blondel has audience of the countess Marguerite, reveals himself, and informs her that Richard's place of confinement, which they have both been searching for so long, is the castle a few yards away. They, along with Sir Williams, arrest Florestan when he comes to see Laurette at the ball given by Williams that night, and the countess' soldiers, led by Blondel, storm the castle. Richard is thus rescued, and Marguerite restored to the arms of her lover.

Of this play by Sedaine three adaptations exist.

a. Richard Coeur de Lion, an historical romance. By General Burgoyne.[38])

This free translation of Sedaine's work was brought out for the first time at Drury Lane in 1786. The „advertisement" of the translator shows its general relation to

---

38) Best known as the British General who surrendered to the Americans at Saratoga in 1777. Wrote for the stage later. The Heiress (1785), a comedy, was popular for some time. Other pieces are The Maid of the Oaks (1774), and The Lord of the Manor (1781). Died 1792.

the original. "In adapting the following scenes to the English stage no adventitious matter has been introduced: some liberty, however, has been taken in effecting the principal incident of the piece; the discovery of Richard's confinement being now given to Matilda in place of Blondel, as well to increase the interest of the situation, as to avoid the less affecting interposition of the heroine in the latter part of the drama. — The elegant author of this Romance will pardon a freedom which has been taken with no other view than that of giving the best assistance of our stage to his admired composition."

Here, as is seen, the heroine's name is changed from Marguerite to Matilda; otherwise, the whole closely follows Sedaine, the music (by M. Grétry) being the same. It is curious to note that just a week before the appearance of Burgoyne's adaptation at Drury Lane another version by a Mr. Mac Nally came out at Covent Garden, without, however, meeting with success.

b. Riccardo cuor di Leone, con Pulcinella guida di un cieco. Napoli 1800.

This is an enlarged form of Sedaine's work, containing a good deal of buffoonery. The motive of love between Florestan and Lauretta is more largely employed in the Italian adaptation. Pulcinella, who has no counterpart in the original French work, is servant to Guglielmo, and also in love with Lauretta. Riccardo, when released, liberally forgives Florestan, whom he takes with him to England along with Lauretta.

c. Richard Coeur de Lion, an historical romance, arranged by Messrs. Maffey for their Theatre of the Petit Lazary at Paris.

This is simply a free English translation of Sedaine, made for the purpose of enabling English theatre-goers unacquainted with the French language better to understand the representation. At the same time a few somewhat objectionable passages are softened down.

4. **La tour ténébreuse et les jours lumineux, contes anglois, par Mlle. l'Héritier de Villandon. Amsterdam 1785.**

The „tour ténébreuse" is only a frame-work used by the authoress in which to set two stories, viz: Ricdin-Ricdon, and La robe de sincerité.

Richard, king of England, having distinguished himself in Palestine, passes in disguise through Germany and suddenly disappears. No trace of him is to be found by his people after sixteen months search, until one day at Linz Blondel de Nesle, who has travelled all over Europe, accidentally hears from his host at an inn of a noble prisoner who was guarded with much care in a tower — la tour ténébreuse — at the entrance to a neighboring wood. Blondel repairs thither and sings before a window the first verse of a song of which Richard had formerly composed the remaining five, he immediately recognizes the voice of the king who responds from within. Blondel succeeds in procuring the position of instructor in singing to the daughter of the gaoler, and in this way gains admission to Richard's presence. The king relates to his faithful minstrel the history of his imprisonment, and tells him how he spent his time composing tales, two of which — the two aboue mentioned — he repeats to Blondel. Their course it is not necessary here to follow. Blondel makes wax impressions of the keys of the prison, and sets out for Vienna. We are left to infer Richard's subsequent liberation.

5. **Walter and William, an historical ballad, translated from the origional poem of Richard Coeur de Lion. Second edition London 1797.**

On the fly-leaf of the copy in the British Museum are written the words: „From the author, viz I. Watts." The ballad consists of 70 4-line stanzas of the following type:

'Twas when athwart the dusky plain
Was thrown the veil of night,
And heroes, wearied out with strife,
Had ceased the lengthened fight.

The work of search amongst dusty volumes of the past is made lighter by the discovery of such amusing productions as the long preface to this poem. The ballad itself is professedly a translation from the German; the original, according to the translator, having been composed by Richard in a German dungeon, — and, contrary to the usage of the royal author, in the German language! Through the kind assistance of a German professor the translator was put in possession of the poem, which had till then lain in obscurity. „The man who attempts to demonstrate an axiom", he says, „commonly concludes his labours with leaving the subject more involved than he found it. Such would be our situation were we to attempt any illustration of the authenticity of this poem. There are some philosophers, whose scepticism has arisen to such a height, that they have disbelieved their own existence."

As far as subject is concerned, this ballad has nothing to do with Richard, except that the two earls, Walter and William, are supposed to have served under him in his wars in Palestine. William leads forth a band of men against the Saracens, and does not return. Walter redoubles his efforts in the war, and searches in vain for his missing brother, until one night the spirit of the latter comes to him, and leads him to a distant castle where the real William lies dead, with his bride, who had killed herself in despair, beside him. Walter had previously had unlawful relations with the girl, and given orders to assassinate her lover. This lover turned out to be William; and Walter was thus in his wickedness himself unconsciously the cause of his brother's death.

6. **Richard the First: a poem. By Sir J. B. Burges. London 1800.**

This very voluminous poem in Spenserian stanzas is divided into 18 Books, containing in all 17,262 lines. The progress of events as here narrated is shortly as follows: During Richard's absence in Palestine the Daemon stirs up revolt in England against those he had left in power at his departure. After a time the news of Richard's wreck and disappearance in Germany is brought back, whereupon Blondel is commissioned by Queen Elinor to set out in search of the king's place of confinement. The minstrel discovers his master in the well-known way, by singing to his harp before the window of the castle, and hearing the response in the familiar voice from within. When Blondel returns to England and reports his success, Elinor summons the nobles of the land to debate measures for obtaining the king's release. One of them, Hubert by name, is sent to the Pope to beg his friendly offices, while Mortimer, Pembroke and Blondel return to the court of Henry of Germany, who holds Richard prisoner, to demand that he be set free. As a result of these messages Richard is brought before the Diet of Worms to answer the charges preferred against him by the duke of Austria, the king of Sicily and others. The royal prisoner, in the course of a very long speech in his own defence, relates the tale of his many adventures, and explains his conduct in the cases in which charges had been made. Daemons, especially the one personifying False Philosophy, prompt Henry to refuse, but after Richard's final powerful plea, and upon the advice of the Prelate of Cologne, he consents to the release. The Daemon False Philosophy now sets on the English people to revolution, whereas Richard uses his persuasion to lead them to be satisfied with the monarchy as upheld in his own person. After the jubilee over Richard's return to England, preparations are made for war against France. In the course of this war Richard, who uses his mighty sword Excaliber, rescues his Queen Berengaria, who had fallen into the hands of his enemies. By the use of the same weapon he overcomes, in a later encounter, king Philip of France, who is borne wounded from the field; but afterwards a reconciliation takes place between the two. Richard returns to Berengaria in England, and Blondel is not forgotten, but is joined with the lady of his heart.

When we consider that the substance of the narrative just given is stretched out to make up an epic over half as long again as Milton's Paradise Lost, we are forced to the conclusion that the author had little of the true poet in him, and was utterly devoid of the faculty of knowing when he had become tedious. The events of history, when he introduces any such, he distorts in a most arbitrary way, while his pompous style of dealing with such lifeless abstractions as the Daemon of False Philosophy has an air of the ludicrous. Posterity has more than confirmed the verdict of a friend who, when the author sent him proof-sheets and asked him for a candid criticism of the poem, advised him to curtail it by at least one-third.

From the higher point of view of the history of civilization this long production has greater worth. It throws a side-light upon the state of feeling in a portion of the English people at that eventful time immediately following the French Revolution. The Daemon of False Philosophy is nothing more than a personification of the revolutionary ideas emanating from France; Richard is the representative of conservatism and the established hereditary monarchy.

7. a. The Lamentation of Queen Elinor. Printed in Evans' Old Ballads II, 78.

This poem of 11 6-line stanzas contains the lament of Queen Elinor, wife of king Henry II of England. She has been imprisoned by him for 16 years owing to the trouble she had caused in his family by her jealousy and maliciousness, and while in durance repents of her maternal shortcomings, acknowledging that she had put out of the way by poison the king's mistress Rosamund. The last two stanzas only have reference to Richard. King Henry's death is finally reported to Queen Elinor in prison.

> But when she heard these tidings told,
> Most bitterly she mourned then;
> Her woful heart she did unfold
> In sight of many noble men.

> And her son Richard being king,
> > From doleful prison did her bring;
> > Who set her for to rule his land,
> > While to Jerusalem he went;
> > And while she had his charge in hand,
> > Her care was great in government,
> > And many prisoners there in hold
> > She set at large from irons cold.

b. A Princely Song of King Richard Cordelion. In Evans' Old Ballads II, 81.

This ballad consists of 22 stanzas of 7 lines, the last line of each stanza constituting a refrain. It begins:
> A noble Christian warrior,
> > King Richard of this land,
> > For fame amongst our worthies brave,
> > Now orderly may stand;
> > The god of battles gave him still
> > A gallant great command,
> > To fight for our Saviour Jesus Christ.

When „fair Jerusalem" lay mourning in heaviness, king Richard with a noble band of knights and gentlemen went forth to its relief.
> But by the way such chances there
> > King Richard did betide,
> > That many of his soldiers
> > For want of victuals died:
> > A new supply this noble king
> > Was forced to provide
> > To fight for etc.

The mighty duke of Austria, to whom he goes for aid, not only refuses all such, but cowardly holds the king prisoner. Richard's followers return to England and
> When they are here providing
> > A ransom for his grace,
> > The duke's own son unreverently
> > King Richard did abase;

For which with one small box o'th'ear
He kill'd him in that place:
In honour of our Saviour etc.

The King is thereupon cast into a dungeon, where a lion is to be let in to him. But the daughter of that duke is moved with gentle pity and enamoured of the prisoner, and comes to his aid.

A rich embroider'd scarf of silk
She secretly convey'd
Into the dungeon where the king
For execution staid;
The which, to save his gentle life,
An instrument was made,
In honour of our Saviour etc.

When the lion approaches, Richard nimbly takes the same, thrusts his arm down the beast's throat, and in sight of the duke and all his lords pulls out its heart. After the performance of this feat Richard is, according to the law of arms, a free man, and returns to England; leaving however, his „dearest love" behind him. Englishmen then muster, and a valiant army is ready to pass the seas to Acon walls. Thus „consuming fire and sword" come into „that country" (apparently the land of the duke of Austria), and cities and towns are laid waste,

Till those the wrongs King Richard had
Were righted by the same.

But the noble King Richard meets with death in the prime of life, by a poisoned shaft. All his „warlike train" make moan for his death; but more than all, „his lady fair" the daughter of the duke, who assigns rich rewards for the discovery of the murderer.

Upon the murtherer (being found)
Much cruelty was shewn;
By her command his skin alive
Was flead from flesh and bone:

And after into dust and air
His body it was thrown,
In honour of our Saviour etc.

But the lady's grief did not end here. Sorrow for Richard broke her heart, she died, and both were buried in one grave.

This interesting ballad is plainly a popular reminiscence of the metrical romance, and we are quite familiar with such points of resemblance as the scarcity of provisions; the killing of the son of the prince that imprisoned Richard by a blow of the fist; the contest with the lion; the love of the daughter of the prince, and the assistance she renders with the scarf; the subsequent revenge of Richard upon his maltreaters; and the method of his death. In the course of time the persons in the romance have become indistinctly separated from each other, and here the duke of Austria also represents the king of Almain. An addition of later times is the love of the princess, her condemnation of Richard's murderer, and her death from a broken heart.

c. **Song by Richard the First, Coeur de Lion, written during his imprisonment in the Tenebreuse, or Black Tower. In Evans' Old Ballads IV, 231.**

This is merely a free and enlarged translation of the French text of Richard's complaint in prison, a version of which in the metre of the original I have already given[39]) This translation is, according to Evans, from the pen of Dr. Burney[40]), and printed in the second volume of the latter's General History of Music. It has no particular merits, and is made heavy by the change to 8-lined stanzas.

---

39) Page 9.
40) Charles Burney (1726—1814). Chiefly known by his General History of Music (1776—89.) Received degree of Doctor of Music from the University of Oxford in 1762. His daughter was the novelist Frances Burney, afterwards Mme. D'Arblay.

The envoi is omitted. It is worthy of note that this „song" of Richard, as announced in the title affixed to the translation, is supposed to have been composed in the „Tenebreuse, or Black Tower", a name which seems to show the translator to have been acquainted with the work of Mlle. L'Héritier de Villandon, La tour ténébreuse, already described.[41])

8. Richard Löwenherz. Ein Gedicht in sieben Büchern.

This long German poem appeared, without the author's name, in a new edition at Berlin, 1819, and published by the Nicolai'sche Buchhandlung. A considerable portion of it is written in rhymed iambic pentameter couplets, though all through the poem the arrangement of the rhymes and the length of the lines vary greatly. As regards the substance of the poem, it is chiefly the creation of the author's imagination, and only follows history in a few scant outlines, as will be seen from the following short analysis.

Book I. King Richard has distinguished himself in the Holy Land, leaving Blondel in England to guard his royal interests. A revolt arises, and Blondel sets out to join his master, but is shipwrecked on the coast of Triest. He finds refuge with a knight named Clifford, now become hermit, who had formerly suffered shipwreck in a similar way. Clifford was a follower of King Richard, and relates to Blondel his adventures.

II. Graf Max von Ottobann, an enemy of Richard in Palestine, stirred up his master, Leopold of Austria, against Richard, and endeavors to induce Leopold to marry his beautiful daughter Ida, against the latter's will. Richard protects her from the profligate duke. On his way home to England Richard is wrecked. Clifford, who is amongst his followers, suceeds in reaching land, but believes King Richard to have been drowned.

---

41) Page 62.

III. Blondel and Clifford soon hear from an old fisherman of a knight whom he had rescued after shipwreck, and who had left him upon his recovery without revealing his name. Believing this to have been King Richard, Blondel and Clifford set out in search of him, parting near Vienna. After two months of search Clifford loses his way in a wood.

IV. Blondel's adventures are now followed from the time of parting from his friend. He comes one day upon a beautiful maiden bathing in a stream deep in a wood. On finding that she is observed the maiden faints, but Blondel rescues her. This maiden, as it turns out, is Ida, who has taken refuge in a cabin in this dense wood with an old companion Walter, in order to escape from her father and duke Leopold.

V. Ida relates her adventures to Blondel. After returning from Palestine Leopold once gave a banquet, at which his praise was sung by many minstrels. Only one song of a dishonorable prince, Ida, and Leopold himself, knew that none other than the giver of the feast was meant. The minstrel is Richard, who is discovered by his proud bearing, and cast into prison, where a lion is let in to devour him — the same lion that Richard had once presented to Leopold as a pledge of friendship in Palestine. The lion is killed by Richard in the usual way, but as it dies it recognises in Richard its former master. Ida faints as she reaches this point of her story. Blondel hastens to fetch water, but on his return to the spot finds that Ida has disappeared.

VI. Ida had fainted at the sight of armed knights led by her father, who had found her place of concealment. While Blondel is fetching water, one of these finds her and leads her to her father. Blondel, like Clifford, strange to say, at this juncture also loses himself in the wood.

VII. The two knights meet at length, for, as it happens, it was on the same night and in the same wood that they had lost their way. After reaching a neighboring castle

Blondel sings before the keep and is answered by King Richard from within. At this moment Graf Max returns to the castle (it is night) with old Walter and Ida, who is about to be given over to the profligate Leopold, when they are fortunately rescued by the bravery of Blondel and Clifford. Graf Max is mortally wounded, but on his death-bed reveals the fact that Clifford is Ida's brother. Afterwards Richard, Blondel, Ida, Clifford and Walter, with their followers, go in haste to Aquileja, where a ship takes them back to England. King Richard is here joyfully welcomed by his people.

Such is the course of this poem, which shows some passages of considerable beauty as subjective verse, but is anything rather than a good epic. It reveals throughout a singular enthusiasm on the part of the author for everything British — a not uncommon thing among his fellow-countrymen and contemporaries of the close of last century.

9. Ivanhoe (1819), and The Talisman (1825). By Sir Walter Scott.

It is hardly necessary to do more than mention in passing that Scott who drew so much from mediaeval sources, also made Richard of the Lion Heart a conspicuous figure in two of his principal novels. Both of these works, Ivanhoe and The Talisman are chiefly interesting in connection with the present theme, as showing Scott's acquaintance with the metrical romance as given in Ellis' synopsis[42]; and the use he made of it in one or two instances. In a note appended to Ivanhoe he thus refers to the precedent for introducing the exchange of blows between Richard and Friar Tuck: — „The interchange of a cuff with the jolly priest is not entirely out of character with Richard I., if romances read him aright. In the very curious romance on

---

42) Ellis, Specimens of Early English Metrical Romances.

the subject of his adventures in the Holy Land, and his return from thence, it is recorded how he exchanged a pugilistic favour of this nature, while a prisoner in Germany. His opponent was the son of his principal warder, and was so imprudent as to give the challenge to this barter of buffets. The king stood forth like a true man, and received a blow which staggered him. In requital, having previously waxed his hand, a practice unknown, I believe, to the gentlemen of the modern fancy, he returned the box on the ear with such interest as to kill his antagonist on the spot. — See, in Ellis's Specimens of English Romance, that of Coeur de Lion."

In the introduction to The Talisman, again, we read the following: — „The most curious register of the history of King Richard is an ancient romance, translated originally from the Norman; and at first certainly having a pretence to be termed a work of chivalry, but latterly becoming stuffed with the most astonishing and monstrous fables. There is, perhaps, no metrical romance upon record, where, along with curious and genuine history, are mingled more absurd and exaggerated incidents. We have placed in the Appendix to this Introduction (see end of Volume) the passage of the romance in which Richard figures as an Ogre, or literal cannibal."

Turning to the appendix alluded to, we find extracts from Ellis, mostly a word-for-word transcription, relating Richard's longing for pork, and his devouring of the Saracens. There is nothing in these references by Scott to lead us to suppose that he was acquainted with the complete romance as printed by Weber in 1810, nine years before the appearance of Ivanhoe.

10. Richard Coeur de Lion, an historical romance. Printed by George Pierce, London.

This anonymous and undated work is a historical novel after the style of Scott. The main story is founded upon actual events in Richard's life, but the writer has at the same time given free scope to his imagination. Sir Thomas de Multon and Sir Fulk D'Oyley appear as the companions of Richard, and the whole story of their imprisonment in Almain, as given here, though the most fabulous of the incidents are omitted, unmistakeably shows an acquaintance on the part of the author with the metrical romance. Richard and his companions are betrayed by a gipsy minstrel. The king's son is called Armour, and, as in the romance, exchanges buffets with Richard, the latter here also employing wax to harden his hand. The king's daughter (here called Priscilla) is enamored of Richard, to rescue whom she even kills the guard, enters the prison, unlocks Richard's fetters, and furnishes him with a dagger. Thus armed, Richard kills the lion in the sight of the king of Almain and his knights. Enraged at the result of the contest, the king is about to have Richard summarily put to death when the duke Leopold of Austria arrives, to whom the prisoner is handed over. Sir Thomas and Sir Fulk are liberated and carry the news over to England, with the result that Richard is at length ransomed and restored to his people.

Both before and after the imprisonment the story follows history more closely. Blondel appears throughout as the attached and faithful follower of Richard, and many songs are introduced as having been sung by the minstrel.

Many features of this story, such as an archery contest in which Locksley appears, remind us of Ivanhoe, and show the whole to be largely an imitation of Scott. The style is not uninteresting, but too many of the incidents related are so fabulous in their nature as to make it impossible for the reader of modern times to take any serious interest in the heroes of them. The edition is richly illustrated with wood-cuts and engravings.

11. Richard Coeur de Lion an historical tragedy. London 1861.

So late as only 30 years ago we find Richard Coeur de Lion made the subject of an English drama. The author, whose name is unknown, was evidently oppressed by the dearth prevailing in the field of dramatic production at that time in England, if we may judge from the following pithy dedication prefixed to his work:
„To the Public.
Time has long made inquiry for an Original Drama. — Is this one?"

Act I gives a picture of Richard's coronation and the plundering of the Jews. The Crusade is preached by one Fulk the Pilgrim. Preparations are made for the Holy Land. Many so-called troubadours' songs (which, however, are all else) are interspersed through this and the following acts.

Act II is made up of the quarrels between Richard and Philip of France in Messina, the coming of Berengaria etc.

Act III gives the arrival in Acres, and subsequent battles with Saladin.

In Act IV the scene is transferred to Vienna. Richard, disguised as a pilgrim, is captured, but while in prison is entertained by the songs of the troubadours. As in the novel just considered, he is brought forth to defend himself before the diet of Worms — also a feature of the poem by Burges.

Act V opens with the joyous celebration of Richard's return by the population of London. Next come warlike operations in Normandy. The final scene is the siege of the castle of Chalous. As Richard lies wounded in his tent Bertram, the archer who had shot him, is brought before him and generously pardoned by the dying king.

Whether it be „original" or not, Time has rightly judged this drama to be of little worth.

Conclusion.

It would add nothing to the completeness of the present theme to enumerate the few other scattered verses of modern writers referring to Richard Coeur de Lion. They are either purely arbitrary creations of the writers and equally applicable to any other hero of the past as to him of the Lion Heart whose fortunes we have been following; or they are mere passing allusions to incidents already fully reviewed in these pages.

To the student of the history and the literature of mediaeval times Richard Coeur de Lion remains one of the most interesting figures, and the light thrown by modern historical research upon his exceptionally eventful career has shown a striking personality, which explains his wide-spread fame amongst his contemporaries and his fabulous name in later generations. He was one of the greatest individualities at a time when fame depended more upon individual greatness than now, and the foremost representative of knighthood when chivalry flourished most. Of the many ways in which posterity has written its recollections of him, it has been the object of these pages to give some account.

The end.

Contents.

		Page
I.	Introduction	3
II.	Richard and Contemporary Troubadour Poetry	7
III.	Metrical Chronicles and Metrical Romances	19
	1. Ambrosius' Histoire de la guerre sainte	19
	2. Konrad of Würzburg's Turnei von Nantheiz	20
	3. Robert of Gloucester's Chronicle	21
	4. Chronicles of Peter of Langtoft and Robert Mannyng	22
	5. The Metrical Romance and its different versions	23
	a) Ms. of Caius College, Cambridge	25
	b) Ms. in Bodleian Library, Douce 228	38
	c) Ms. in British Museum, Additional 31,042	42
	d) Ms. in British Museum, Harley 4690	46
	e) Auchinleck Ms.	48
	f) Wynkyn de Worde's Printed Copy	50
IV.	Later works in chronological order	56
	1. Troublesome Raigne of John	56
	2. The Tragedy of Richard I.	58
	3. Richard Coeur de Lion. Comedy by Sedaine	59
	a) Burgoyne's Translation of the foregoing work	60
	b) Riccardo cuor di Leone	61
	c) Richard Coeur de Lion, arranged by Messrs. Maffey	61
	4. La tour ténébreuse, by Mlle. L'Héritier de Villandon	62
	5. Walter and William	62
	6. Richard the First. By Sir J. B. Burges	63
	7. a) Lamentation of Queen Elinor	65
	b) Princely Song of King Richard	66
	c) Song by Richard the First	68
	8. Richard Löwenherz. Ein Gedicht	69
	9. Ivanhoe and The Talisman	71
	10. Richard Coeur de Lion, an historical romance	72
	11. Richard Coeur de Lion, an historical tragedy	74
V.	Conclusion	75

www.ingramcontent.com/pod-product-compliance
Lightning Source LLC
Chambersburg PA
CBHW020231090426
42735CB00010B/1648